THE GREAT AWAKENING:
EVENT AND EXEGESIS

PROBLEMS IN AMERICAN HISTORY

EDITOR

LOREN BARITZ

State University of New York, Albany

THE NATURE OF LINCOLN'S LEADERSHIP
Donald E. Fehrenbacher

THE AMERICAN CONSTITUTION
Paul Goodman

THE AMERICAN REVOLUTION
Richard J. Hooker

AMERICA IN THE COLD WAR
Walter LaFeber

ORIGINS OF THE COLD WAR, 1941–1947
Walter LaFeber

AMERICAN IMPERIALISM IN 1898
Richard H. Miller

TENSIONS IN AMERICAN PURITANISM
Richard Reinitz

THE GREAT AWAKENING
Darrett B. Rutman

WORLD WAR I AT HOME
David F. Trask

THE CRITICAL YEARS,
AMERICAN FOREIGN POLICY, 1793–1825
Patrick C. T. White

THE GREAT AWAKENING

Event and Exegesis

EDITED BY

DARRETT B. RUTMAN

The University of New Hampshire

John Wiley & Sons, Inc.

New York • *London* • *Sydney* • *Toronto*

Library of Congress Catalogue Card Number 79–110174

Cloth: SBN 471 74725 4   Paper: SBN 471 74726 2

Printed in the United States of America

10 9 8 7 6 5 4 3 2 1

SERIES PREFACE

This series is an introduction to the most important problems in the writing and study of American history. Some of these problems have been the subject of debate and argument for a long time, although others only recently have been recognized as controversial. However, in every case, the student will find a vital topic, an understanding of which will deepen his knowledge of social change in America.

The scholars who introduce and edit the books in this series are teaching historians who have written history in the same general area as their individual books. Many of them are leading scholars in their fields, and all have done important work in the collective search for better historical understanding.

Because of the talent and the specialized knowledge of the individual editors, a rigid editorial format has not been imposed on them. For example, some of the editors believe that primary source material is necessary to their subjects. Some believe that their material should be arranged to show conflicting interpretations. Others have decided to use the selected materials as evidence for their own interpretations. The individual editors have been given the freedom to handle their books in the way that their own experience and knowledge indicate is best. The overall result is a series built up from the individual decisions of working scholars in the various fields, rather than one that conforms to a uniform editorial decision.

A common goal (rather than a shared technique) is the bridge of this series. There is always the desire to bring the reader as close to these problems as possible. One result of this objective is an emphasis of the nature and consequences of problems and events, with a de-emphasis of the more purely historiographical issues. The goal is to involve the student in the reality of crisis, the inevitability of ambiguity, and the excitement of finding a way through the historical maze.

Above all, this series is designed to show students how experienced historians read and reason. Although health is not contagious, intellectual engagement may be. If we show students something significant in a phrase or a passage that they otherwise may have missed, we will have accomplished part of our objective. When students see something that passed us by, then the process will have been made whole. This active and mutual involvement of editor and reader with a significant human problem will rescue the study of history from the smell and feel of dust.

Loren Baritz

CONTENTS

INTRODUCTION

What was the Great Awakening? In the calm of his study, the academician answers easily. He first admits that definitions are arbitrary, that in this particular case scholars have assigned various initial and terminal dates, but that he feels the most viable definition is the period of religious excitement and fervor in the English colonies in America that began with the arrival in Philadelphia in late 1739 of George Whitefield, "the great itinerant" as he has been called, and ended in roughly 1744 when the religious fervor began giving way to a period of institutional and intellectual retrenchment on the part of the ministry most involved in the Awakening.

The academician's language, however, hardly catches the heated emotions, the deep fears, the hopes grounded on even deeper beliefs, and the despair and ecstasy of a time when, as one observer noted, "the Sight and Noise of Lamentation, seem'd a little Resemblance of what we may imagine will be when the great Judge pronounces the tremendous Sentence of, *Go ye cursed into everlasting Fire.*" And yet this depth of emotion has to be conveyed if the Awakening is to be defined at all.

Moreover, a definition so constricted by dates initial and terminal hardly satisfies the necessity of seeing the event in a total context. The religious scene in the early eighteenth century colonies was multifaceted, of course—Virginia nominally Anglican, New England basically Congregationalist, and the middle colonies (especially Pennsylvania) of mixed persuasions. But the basic religious tone, common throughout, was one of comfortable complacency among both laymen and ministers. The great burning question of the Reformation, carried to America in the early seventeenth century, was in the past and had been

1

for some time. Such a complacent scene was fertile ground for
emotional religious revivals stirred early by Solomon Stoddard,
Jonathan Edwards, Theodore Frelinghuysen, and Gilbert Tennent, and finally set raging as *the* Awakening by the great itinerant himself. The question these ministers of the gospel insisted on asking was the burning one of the Reformation all
over again: "Are you God's servant or merely a man among
men?"—a question transmuted by laymen into a simpler "Am I
saved?" But in the process of asking, the Awakeners revived
and reinforced a whole set of attitudes with such vehemence
and effect that one can argue that they left lasting marks on
American society long after the religious enthusiasm had waned.
What were the components of the set? Evangelical religiosity,
certainly; super-righteousness and super-morality from a godly,
not a social, point of view; perfectionism—the preparation of
mankind, and more particularly, of mankind in America, for the
coming of Christ's Kingdom; and the intrinsic negative factors:
disdain for rationalism, compromise, and social attitudes developed out of human experience rather than derived from God.

Once the Awakening is defined, a second—and most proper—
question arises. What is its relevance to the contemporary
American? In other words, why read about it? And specifically,
why read about it in the form in which the Awakening is presented in this volume—a book of readings, one half of which,
using the words of the time, tells the story of the event from its
setting to its aftermath, the other half being devoted to what historians have written about it? One can suggest three related
points of relevance.

First, there is the general caveat, "history does not say—im-
mutably!" History is not the "Good Book" of the past, written
once and for all ages. It is, rather, a tenuous series of interpretations based upon a few words (such as those presented here
in Part I) and, in some cases, artifacts, that managed to escape
destruction in a past time and survive to that time in which the
historian is writing. The constant appeal to the past—the states-
man, politician, demagogue, or editorialist pointing to the noble
or ignoble past with the phrase (or one of its many variants)
"History proves . . ."—can and should be immediately dismissed

by simply asking "Whose history?" or "History as written by what historian?" "History proves," for example, "that the doctrine of predestination and the ideals of the American republic are incompatible!" My historian in this case is Vernon L. Parrington in his *Main Currents of American Thought,* a part of which is included in Part II. But: "History proves that predestination and American ideas *are* compatible, indeed, that American ideals emanate largely from those who believed most firmly in predestination." My historian is Alan Heimert in the selection from his *Religion and the American Mind: From the Great Awakening to the Revolution.*

Second, there is the relevance of the study of the Great Awakening to the general problem of relating ideas and actions. From one standpoint, this is a strictly methodological problem applicable to historians. If history is a tenuous series of interpretations based upon words and artifacts surviving from one time to another, then it follows that the interpretation of a historian devolves from the specific words and artifacts that he chooses. In the main, what is left of a past age tends to fall into either one or the other of two categories, first what is termed by some "ideational material" (that is, the writings of the elite, the educated, and the intellectual leaders of the past culture), and second, the records that give indication of actions (government and court records, church records, and the like). The historian utilizing ideational material will very often draw a quite different picture from that drawn by a historian using "action" or "real" material. Most of the history of the Great Awakening has been based upon ideational material—Parrington, Heimert, Perry Miller, and Richard L. Bushman, to use examples included among the selections which follow; only recently have historians concerned with the Awakening begun using action material, in this volume the example being the article by J. M. Bumsted. Yet the difference between ideal and real is more than merely methodological, for consider the nature of the world we live in. Is it not one in which ideals and realities exist at least in juxtaposition and frequently in opposition?—a point to which we will return.

Third, the Awakening can be considered relevant because of its part in the process of making Americans what they are today. This can be approached in any number of ways, as it is in the various selections of Part II. That from the work of Alan Heimert emphasizes the role of the Awakening in preparing the American mind for the Revolution and Republicanism. Those from the writings of Perry Miller and Richard L. Bushman accent the effects upon the very fabric of society—both scholars, from different viewpoints, arguing that in the Awakening, European notions of the nature of social authority tended to be replaced by inherently American notions. Dietmar Rothermund, looking at the Awakening from the standpoint of ecclesiology, notes a peculiar American sense of denomination emerging. And in the selection from the work of H. Richard Niebuhr the concept of a peculiar mission for America as it was found in the Awakening and moved into the American mind is accented.

Which element of Americanization is to be stressed is a matter of interpretation, hence for the reader a matter of informed choice. And indeed, in the light of the specific caveat offered via the selection from Leonard J. Trinterud—who sees the differences between Awakeners and their foes within Presbyterianism ultimately negligible—and the general caveat offered via the work of J. M. Bumsted and susceptible to an extreme application, one might conceivably argue against Americanization *in toto,* and with that against the contemporary relevance of any study of the Great Awakening.

History is tenuous interpretation! Historians differ! Contemporary relevance depends upon the specific interpretation! This is, indeed, slippery ground for the reader. But it is exactly here that the historian can be of use. If what he has to say is offered and accepted as merely informed opinion, he can serve as a guide, not only to the past but to the relevance of the past to the present. With this understanding, therefore—offered by me as a historian and hence subject to acceptance, amendment, or rejection by the reader—I point to the concept of American mission discernible in the perfectionism of the awakeners, and in their insistence upon the coming of Christ's Kingdom and the necessity for preparing for it.

A sense of mission—more often than not, a messianic mission, a mission to save or guide the world—seems to be a cardinal thread running through the American past. Everywhere as we glance about our past we see the American or (in the colonial period) the proto-American almost painfully aware of playing a world-shaking role. John Winthrop, the leader of the 1630 migration that settled Massachusetts Bay, says, for example:

"Wee must Consider that wee shall be as a Citty upon a Hill, the eies of all people are uppon us; soe that if wee shall deale falsely with our god in this worke wee have undertaken and soe cause him to withdrawe his present help from us, wee shall be made a story and a by-word through the world."

In the very declaration of American independence, "a decent respect to the opinions of mankind" required the rebels to "declare the causes which impel them to the separation"—no thought here that perhaps the mind of mankind in, say, Austria or Denmark or the farther regions of Hindustan was *not* directed toward America. In the 1860s, the Americans could not have a tidy little rebellion important only for its effect on their own national existence—the sort of rebellion the English had so frequently in Scotland and Ireland; ours had to be "a great civil war, testing" fundamental concepts vital to the whole world, a world that could "never forget what" brave Union soldiers did at Gettysburg. America could not fight for mundane goals in 1898 or 1917—in the latter case, of course, we fought to make the world safe for democracy. Even World War II, in many ways our most realistic of wars, had its missionary aspect, while since then we have taken to ourselves the role of moral policeman for the world and guardian of what some have termed a mystical, ill-defined "free world."

The contemporary relevance of this seems clear enough. Those who would redefine America's present attitude toward the world must well realize the weight of tradition that lies behind that attitude—*ergo*, the stamina of the ideas they stand against—and perhaps at no other time was the tradition so resoundingly verbalized as in the Great Awakening. "This new world," Jonathan

Edwards wrote, was probably discovered "that God might in it begin a new world in a spiritual respect, when he creates the *new heavens* and *new earth.*" And those who would effect a redefinition and who argue in moralistic terms—*viz.,* that it is immoral for America to be the world's guardian or (as they see it) to define in terms dictated by self-interest that intangible "free world"—must be aware too of the tradition that weighs *them* down, for the reverse of the coin emblazoned with the concept of mission bears the concept of moral America. In order to be worthy of the mission assigned her, America must be pure and faultless—again a point clear in the Awakening and in the zeal for moral reform inspired by it. Either way the contemporary American turns—if he argues for the guardian role against the black nemesis of communism (can we cast back to the eighteenth century and read "Devil"?) or for the abandonment of the guardianship as immoral—he is involved with cardinal traditions.

I am aware of a fundamental criticism of this general interpretation of America as a land moved by ideals; that is, the criticism inherent in the tenuous relationship between verbalized ideas and actions. I am particularly aware of it, inasmuch as most of my own work as a historian has been devoted to the early years of the seventeenth century when, to my eyes, the contrast between ideational rhetoric and reality was so great. But I suggest that there is a way around the criticism. I would postulate that the very weight of rhetoric, over time, has resulted in the growing conviction that the rhetoric is reality. With regard to the idea of mission, for example, I suggest that the great bulk of migrants who journeyed with Winthrop to Massachusetts Bay in 1630 were *not* moved to act by the ideal that he expressed, although the rhetoric of the ideal was clearly there. Similarly, actions were perhaps not the result of ideas in many instances in the Awakening, as Bumsted points out, although the ideas were clearly there. But future generations, listening to the rhetoric of the past (to some extent, historian David W. Noble has suggested, through the works of historians) and repeating it for themselves, over time, convinced themselves that the rhetoric was indeed the cause of the early act, and hence themselves were more likely to act upon that rhetoric. The process can be diagrammed as an inverted pyramid (representing the ideational rhetoric or ideal considerations) becoming more and more dominant *vis á vis* real considerations over time (Figure 1).

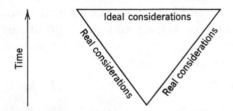

Of course, real considerations never have lost and never will lose their force completely. But one can postulate further that the force of real considerations as against ideal considerations in making public (even private) decisions correlates with the degree of abstraction of the action to be decided. Foreign policy (in the American mind) can be dominated by ideal considerations because, in the main, the effect is remote. Domestic policy, being more immediate, is subject to a greater extent to real considerations. There is, for example, little to stand in the way of being the guardian of the free world when it does not cost very much (although when the responsibilities of being the guardian result in higher taxes, there is the possibility that people will object). On the other hand, the moral argument for domestic reform, the assimilation of the black, for example, finds hard going in a real situation. To use a crude but classic example: there is the good citizen who vows that the black man must be treated with justice and morality until he is asked to accept a black man as his neighbor—at which time all of the tales of black men and real estate values come into play. This last suggests, too, a fundamental fact about the contemporary scene. Mission and morality have been the heritage of the white Anglo-Saxon Protestant (and those assimilated into W.A.S.P. society over time); the black man has been a victim of the mission. White America, consequently, can expect that morality will prevail as an act of faith in the historic mission and insist on law and order in the meantime as a practical (or real) matter; the black man can doubt the act of faith and resort to action in consideration only of the real situation.

But we have come a long way from the subject at hand, the Great Awakening. The point is simply that contemporary concerns or problems cannot be seen completely in the vacuum of today but must be placed in the context of a total past, and the suggestion is that the Awakening and the sense of mission inherent in it—far from being things solely of the past—may well have much to tell us about ourselves.

PART ONE
The Event

THE SETTING

1   *Hugh Jones: The Present*
     State of Virginia (1742)

From the vantage point of the pulpit, the early decades of the eighteenth century were marked by materialism and secularism; earthly, not heavenly, goals were sought by men. The Rev. Hugh Jones (ca. 1670–1760), teaching mathematics at the College of William and Mary in Williamsburg from 1716 to 1721 and lecturing occasionally at Bruton Parish church, was not one to fight these tendencies in the Anglican establishment of Virginia. But in his account of the colony written on his return to England, and in particular in his recommendations for the church, he inadvertently—but well—described them, for here is a tone of absolute, almost gutless, neutrality. The median minister was wanted to preach to median men. Beyond this, however, he displayed an Anglican concern for the forms of religion—lamenting, for example, the lack of proper communion utensils, a proper episcopal establishment—and gave little thought to the spirit.

It is an opinion as erroneous as common, that any sort of clergymen will serve in Virginia; for persons of immoral lives, or weak parts and mean learning, not only expose themselves, but do great prejudice to the propagation of the gospel there; and

SOURCE. Hugh Jones, *The Present State of Virginia* . . . (London: J. Clarke, 1742), edited by Richard L. Morton, Chapel Hill: University of North Carolina Press for the Virginia Historical Society, 1956, pp. 117–122. Reprinted by permission of The University Press of Virginia and the editor.

by bad arguments or worse example, instead of promoting religion, become encouragers of vice, profaneness, and immorality. . . . Neither do they want quarrelsom and litigious ministers, who would differ with their parishioners about insignificant trifles, who had better stay at home and wrangle with their own parishes. . . . Neither would they have meer scholars and stoicks, or zealots too rigid in outward appearance, as they would be without loose and licentious profligates; these do damage to themselves, to others, and to religion.

And as in words and actions they should be neither too reserved nor too extravagant; so in principles should they be neither too high nor too low: The Virginians being neither favourers of popery nor the Pretender on the one side, nor of presbytery nor anarchy on the other; but are firm adherents to the present constitution in state, the Hanover succession and the Episcopal Church of England as by law established; consequently then if these are the inclinations of the people, their ministers ought to be of the same sentiments, equally averse to papistical and schismatical doctrines, and equally free from Jacobitish and Oliverian tenets. These I confess are my principles, and such as the Virginians best relish, and what every good clergyman and true Englishman (I hope) will favour; for such will never refuse to say with me

> God bless the Church, and George its defender,
> Convert the fanaticks, and baulk the Pretender.

For our sovereign is undoubtedly the defender and head of our national Church of England, in which respect we may pray for the King and Church; but Christ is the head of the universal or catholick Church, in which respect we wish prosperity to the Church and King.

Clergymen for Virginia should be of such parts, tempers, and notions as these. They likewise should be persons that have read and seen something more of the world, than what is requisite for an English parish; they must be such as can converse and know more than bare philosophy and speculative ethicks, and have studied men and business in some measure as well as books; they may act like gentlemen, and be facetious and good-humoured, without too much freedom and licentiousness; they may be good scholars without becoming cynicks, as they may be good Christians without appearing stoicks. They should be such as will give up a small matter rather than create disturbance and mischief; for in all parishes the minister as well as the people should pass by some little things, or else by being at variance the best preaching may have the worst effect; yet they must not condescend too far, nor part with a material right, but must be truly zealous and firm in every good cause both publick and private. There are many such worthy, prudent, and pious clergymen as these in Virginia, who meet with the love, reputation, respect, and encouragement that such good men may deserve and expect: However, there have been some whose learning, actions, and manners have not been so good as might be wished; and others by their outward behaviour have been suspected to have been, some Jacobites, and others Presbyterians inwardly in their hearts.

In Virginia there is no ecclesiastical court, so that vice, prophaneness, and immorality are not suppressed so much as might be: The people hate the very name of the bishop's court. There are no visitations, so that the churches are often not in the best repair, nor as decently adorned as might be; neither in some places can the Lord's Supper be administered with such holy reverence as it should be, for want of proper materials and utensils. The churches being not consecrated are not entered with such reverent demeanour, as ought to be used in God's holy tabernacle.

For want of confirmation persons are admitted to the Holy Sacrament with mean and blind knowledge, and poor notions of the divine mysteries of the Supper of the Lord; which is an abuse of a thing so very sacred.

In North Carolina and several parts of Virginia children are often neglected to be baptized till they are grown up, and then perhaps may never know or never mind that they want to be christened; and many esteem it unnecessary.

The clerks upon several occasions performing too great a share of divine services, expose the Church to shame and danger, and often bring contempt and disdain upon the persons and function of the ministers.

Ministers are often obliged to bury in orchards, and preach funeral sermons in houses, where they also generally marry and christen; and as for weddings there is no regard to the time of the day nor the season of the year; and in North Carolina the justices marry.

Now to remedy all these grievances and deficiencies, with all evils of the like kind, there is an absolute necessity for a person whose office upon this occasion should be somewhat uncommon, till a bishop be established in those parts; who might pave out a way for the introduction of mitres into the English America, so greatly wanting there. This person should have instructions and power for discharging such parts of the office, of a bishop, of a dean, and of an arch-deacon, as necessity requires, and the nature of those sacred functions will permit; and from a medium of these three functions he might be called Dean of Virginia; under whose jurisdiction North Carolina might fall for the present, till the constitution in church and state there be better advanced. . . .

Such a person as this might do a vast deal of good, and reduce the church discipline in Virginia to a much better method than at present it is in: For though the church of England be there established, yet by permitting too great liberty, and by being too indifferent in many such respects as are here specified, great inconveniences have arose; and we may certainly expect far greater detriment in the Church from hence, unless timely lenitives and proper remedies be applied, in the best methods that can possibly be devised; some such methods (I conceive) as these here proposed may not be esteemed least proper; and if they be rejected or despised, yet I am persuaded that they are not so insignificant as some may imagine, and not altogether so despicable as to be quite disregarded; and not thought worthy of the serious perusal of any concerned in affairs of this nature.

2   *Samuel Wigglesworth*
        An Essay for Reviving Religion (1733)

New England's ministry, too, looked on the land and saw spiritual desolation. But unlike the Virginians, they were never mute. The jeremiad—that peculiar sermon form that took its name from the lamentations of the prophet Jeremiah—had come to New England with the ministers of the first generation, fallen into disuse during the heady early years of religious ardor, and been revived as ardor seemed to diminish. More often than not, the Jeremiad sermons were merely ritual flagellations—denunciations of the sinfulness of society and threats of God's vengeance for falling away from the good ways of the first generation. Minister Samuel Wigglesworth (1688–1768), delivering the Boston election-day sermon in 1733, went farther. To the flagellation he added an implicit criticism of the ministry itself and a call for ministerial action. Prompting the criticism was a cardinal element of the age, the resort to reason, and its religious concomitant. In the minds of educated men, authority no longer held sway; it was not enough to say "it has been written" in order to prove something. Men, to believe, had to be convinced by "the light of reason." Among ministers, even in New England, there was a softening of the old Jehovah, the God wrathful without reason (at least to men). The new God was gentle, loving, easily served. Wigglesworth—and there were others—was not less educated, certainly, but he was unconvinced of the new nature of God and would have man's duty toward an absolute deity expounded.

It is a Truth, that we have a *goodly exterior Form of Religion;* Our *Doctrine, Worship* and *Sacraments* are *Orthodox, Scriptural* and *Divine.* There is an external Honour paid to the *Sabbath;* and a professed Veneration for Christ's *Ambassadors* for the

SOURCE. Samuel Wigglesworth, *An Essay for Reviving Religion. A Sermon Delivered at Boston . . . May 30, MDCCXXXIII,* Boston: S. Kneeland for D. Henchman, 1733, pp. 22–26, 30–31.

sake of their Lord. We set up and maintain the *Publick Worship* of God, and the Voice of the Multitude saying, *Let us go into the House of the Lord,* is yet heard in our Land.

Moreover *Practical Religion* is not quite extirpated among us, and there are, it is to be hoped, a considerable number of serious and vigorous Christians in our Churches, whose *Piety* is acknowledged and respected by their Neighbours, whilst Living; and their *Memories* preserved for it when deceased. Whilst on the other hand, the *prophane and wicked Person* is generally abhor'd; and the more deformed Vices seek the retreats of Darkness to hide their detestable heads.

And yet with what sorrow must we speak, that these things are but the *Remains* of what we *Once* might show; the shadow of past and vanish'd Glory! . . .

If the *Fear of the Lord* be to *Hate Evil,* as *Prov.* 8. 13. Then it is to be feared that our *Religion runs low,* and but little of this Fear is in us: Inasmuch as we find our selves stained with so many most odious Vices, especially *Uncleanness, Drunkenness, Theft, Covetousness, Violence, Malice, Strife,* and others: Which tho', as 'twas said before, they be look'd upon with dishonour, yet multitudes are found who are not ashamed to commit them; and where such *Iniquities abound,* may we not infer that *the Love of many waxeth cold?*

Again, *How Weak is the Testimony that is born by our Good Men against those Transgressions!* Ought not holy Ones when they *Behold the Transgressor, to be grieved!* Will they not hate the things which God hates, and express a suitable indignation at the presumption of the Wicked, and the affronts which they put upon the Majesty of Heaven? *Reproving,* and bringing them to *Punishment?* If therefore our *Professors of Religion* think *Open Prophaneness* unworthy of their Wrath: If our *Ministers of Religion* are sparing to bear their publick Testimony against it; and when also the *Ministers of Justice* are too Complaisant to the Sons of Wickedness, to Execute the wholesome Laws of the Province upon them; unto how low an ebb is our Goodness come! . . .

Nor is it less evident that many of us who have given our *Consent to Religion;* are for *Curtailing* and *Abridging* it as much as we can: contenting ourselves with the *lowest degrees* of it, and carefully avoiding all it's most *Arduous, Mortifying Duties,* such as *Mortification* of our *Beloved Lusts, Self-Denial, Weaning ourselves from the World, Bestowing our Riches on Works of Piety,* and *Overcoming Evil with Good:* As if we were resolved not to *Wrestle with Flesh and Blood,* and to make *Christ's Yoke lighter* than Himself hath done? Many Men are upon Enquiry, *What strict Duty requires of them,* How often they must *Pray,* How often going to *Meeting* will serve the turn; and if they can satisfy their *Conscience,* they care not how seldom: How far *Christian Liberty* may be *extended,* and whither they may not take this or that *Gratification consistently with Religion?* How *sunk* and *debas'd a Temper* is this! And yet 'tis too evidently our own to be deny'd. . . .

I shall only now add, That the *Powerful Love of the World, and Exorbitant Reach after Riches,* which is become the reigning Temper in Persons of all Ranks in our Land, is alone enough to awaken our concerns for abandon'd, slighted and forgotten Religion. 'Tis this that takes up our Time, seizes our Affections, and governs our Views: Straitens our Hands; respecting Works of Charity, and pusheth us into the most wicked Schemes and Methods. . . . This *Worldly Spirit* has in a great measure thrust out Religion, and given it a *Wound* which will prove *Deadly* unless infinite Mercy prevent. . . .

It is to be hoped that things have not yet run to so low an ebb with us, but that a good number, if not the greater part of our *Priests* are seen *Cloathed with Righteousness;* That the good and amiable things which they press upon their Hearers are in some good measure to be found in their own *Personal Characters.* If this be one of the Good things which remain, Let us (my Fathers & Brethren in the Ministry) strengthen it by a more universal Care to live our own Sermons: That we may *Adorn the Doctrine of God our Saviour,* by a *Conversation,* which may convince the World that we believe what we preach, & relish the Duties which we perswade others to embrace. Incredible will be the Influence of such an *Harmony* between our *Doctrine and Life* in setting a new face upon Religion. In such a case, we might reasonably hope, that we should not *Labour in vain nor spend our strength for nought.*

And then as to our *Preaching,* Let us not labour to build up a *Shell,* to form a meer *Carcase of Godliness,* by furnishing our Auditors with *Moral Virtues,* only, void of *Internal Vital Principles;* but *Travail in Birth* with them until *Christ be formed in them,* and they are become holy in Heart, as well as blameless of Life. I know not how we can begin with out Flocks better, than the *Great Prophet & Teacher* did with *Nicodemus, Except a Man be born again, he cannot see the Kingdom of God.*

Our Reasoning with them must tend to perswade them to be *Real and Altogether,* not *Almost Christians,* and therefore we must not heal their wounded Consciences slightly; but wisely suffer *Convictions* to ripen into true *Conversion:* That they may pass from *Death* to *Life* in good Earnest, and not deceive themselves with vain Hopes, and impose upon the World with their *Name* that they *Live.* To prevent which also the Duty of Self-Examination, ought to be frequently urg'd upon them, that they may judge of their state, and rectify what is amiss.

3   Solomon Stoddard
A Guide to Christ (1714)

What Wigglesworth called for in Boston in 1733, the Rev. Solomon Stoddard (1643–1729) had for long been practicing in Northampton, Massachusetts. Stoddard is known principally for his opening of communion in Northampton to church members and nonmembers alike in contravention of a traditional limitation of communion to full members, and for his attempt to create a presbyterian-type church organization. Yet he was above all else an evangelist. In opening communion he was motivated by his view that the church should be less

SOURCE. Solomon Stoddard, *A Guide to Christ, or, The Way of Directing Souls That are Under the Work of Conversion. Compiled for the Help of Young Ministers, and May be Serviceable to Private Christians, Who Are Enquiring the Way to Zion,* Boston: J. Allen for N. Boone, 1714, pp. 1–4.

a haven for the elect in a sea of sinners and more a tool by which men might be brought to God. In espousing a presbyterian polity, he was moved by a distrust of traditional congregationalism, which put church power in the hands of mere men, and by his desire to erect a system by which the quality of the ministry might be better controlled. In 1714, as part of his attempt to create an evangelistic ministry throughout New England and particularly in his own Connecticut River Valley, he prepared a handbook, in essence a practical guide for "directing souls," in which he tersely set forth what the good minister must do and what must be left for God to do—a distinction drawn from Calvinistic theology that must be understood if the ministerial role in the coming Awakening is to be understood.

The work of *Regeneration* being of absolute necessity unto salvation, it greatly concerns ministers especially, in all ways possible, to promote the same and in particular that they guide souls aright who are under a work of *preparation.* Some there be that do deny any necessity of the *preparatory* work of the spirit of God, in order to a closing with Christ. This is a very dark cloud, both as it is an evidence that such men have not the experience of that work in their own souls, and as it is a sign that such men are utterly unskilful in guiding others that are under this work. If this *opinion* should prevail in the land, it would give a deadly wound to religion. It would expose men to think themselves converted when they are not. . . .

The work of preparation does not make the work of the new creation the easier, for after men have a work of preparation, sin reigns in them as much as before. Preparation does not at all destroy the principle [of God's grace], and men, when prepared, can do nothing to help God in planting grace in them, and men, that are not prepared, can do nothing to hinder God in implanting grace. But yet it is very agreeable to reason, that the spirit do a work of preparation, before it does infuse grace. [And] it is the duty of ministers to preach such things as are proper to work this preparation. They are bound to preach the *threatenings of the law,* man's *insufficiency,* and God's *sovereignty.* Yea, the manner of God is to deal with men after the manner of men. Man is a rational creature, and therefore God deals with

him in a moral way, sets convictions before him. Men would
make enemies submit, before they pardon them; so does
God. . . .

And seeing there is such a work of *preparation* foregoing
men's *closing with Christ,* it must needs be of great consequence
for awakened sinners to be guided aright under this work. If
men have the best guides, yet they may miscarry, but undoubtedly many do perish for want of suitable help. Some after they
have been in trouble a while do grow *discouraged,* under apprehensions that their seeking will be in vain, and so leave off
endeavoring after a converted estate. Some *wander* up and down
under fears and hopes, as the children of Israel in the Wilderness,
until they die. They cannot be quiet in a way of sin, neither
can they find the way of deliverance. And many others, after a
little trouble, are *comforted* under a notion of being at peace
with God. Unskilful *Surgeons* make a palliate cure, and persuade them that the bitterness of death is past. Multitudes of
souls perish through the ignorance of those that should guide
them in the way to heaven; men are nourished up with vain
hopes of being in a state of salvation, before they have got half
the way to Christ.

Those therefore whose business is to lead souls to Christ, had
need furnish themselves with skill and understanding to handle
wounded consciences in a right manner. . . . There are two
things especially serviceable to this end.

One is, that they *get experience of this word in their own
hearts.* If they have no experience, they will be but *blind
guides.* . . . Whatever books men have read, there is great need
of *experimental* knowledge in a minister. Many particular things
will occur that he will not meet withal in books. It is a great
calamity to wounded consciences, to be under the direction of
an unexperienced minister.

The *other* is *to be acquainted with the observations of those
who have travelled much in this work.* If a man have experience in his own soul, that will not reach all cases that may
come before him. There is great variety in the workings of the
spirit and in the workings of men's hearts (under the conviction

of the Spirit), and men, that have had to do with many souls in their distresses, may afterwards meet with such difficulties as may puzzle them very much. . . . This small *Treatise*, composed upon the desire of some *younger ministers*, is offered to the consideration of such as do desire to be further instructed in the right way of dealing with distressed souls. And if the author shall be hereby the instrument of the salvation of any perishing souls, he shall count his labor well bestowed.

4
Gilbert Tennent
The Unsearchable Riches of Christ (1737)

What is happiness? Is it the accumulation of honors? Pleasure? Riches? No!—although too many men act as if the answer were yes. Happiness, rather, is the state of "grace and Glory" that is to be found through Christ. So argued the Rev. Gilbert Tennent (1703–1764), reflecting not only his own thought but also his view of the primary but futile pursuits of the leaders of his society. The son of the Rev. William Tennent—himself an ardent minister and educator of ardent ministers at his Neshaminy, Pennsylvania "Log College"—Tennent was a Presbyterian minister in New Brunswick, New Jersey, deeply involved in the recurrent local revivals that marked the Delaware Valley and New Jersey plains from the arrival of the Rev. Theodore J. Frelinghuysen in 1719.

The Desire of Happiness is co-natural to the human Soul, and yet remains with it, notwithstanding the Ruins of its Apostacy from the blessed GOD.

SOURCE. Gilbert Tennent, "The Unsearchable Riches of Christ Considered in Two Sermons on Ephes. iii. 8. Prech'd at New-Brunswick in August, 1737," in *Sermons on Sacramental Occasions by Divers Ministers*, Boston: J. Draper for D. Henchman, 1739, pp. i–v.

But alass, such brutal Blindness infatuates the Understandings, and such sensual Pravity byasses the Wills of the most; that they pursue wrong Measures to attain the Happiness they desire.

Some of a lofty Genius, with unwearied Assiduity, labour to secure Honours, thinking therein to obtain Happiness; and to that End they climb the aspiring Top of *Parnassus*, emaciate their Bodies, and waste their animal Spirits in long and deep Studies, thinking by their labour'd and learn'd Lucubrations, to spread and eternize their Fame. Others for the same Purpose, boldly tread the Crimson Fields of War, fearlessly open their senseless Bosoms to all the numerous Engines and sudden Avenues of pregnant Dangers, and of cruel Deaths, thinking themselves great Gainers, if through the Loss of their Lives, they can secure martial Honours and perpetuate Renown for their heroick Bravery, in the Records of Fame. But alass! how much is the unhappy Simplicity of those gallant Souls to be pity'd! for what Good can martial Glory do to the dead?

Others by deeper but securer Policies, & more ungenerous Methods, seek to mount the Wings of Honour, and reach the highest Pinacle of Fame, by labouring to enhance great Places in the Church and State, through the softest Flatteries and most subtil Stratagems; Methods to be abhorr'd by every honest and ingenious Mind. But when Men have obtain'd Honour, what is it? It is neither a substantial, nor a durable Good; it cannot make us good or happy; it may indeed *corrupt* us, by elating our Pride; but it can never *content* us: We may as easily grasp an Arm full of our own Shadow, as content our Minds with Fame; and as it is a meer empty Bubble in its Nature, and often corrupting in its Effects; so it is various and vanishing in its Continuance, as fickle as the Wind.

Some on the contrary of a baser Temper, and meaner Mould, being void of every Thing sublime or noble, dreaming that Happiness is to be had in terrene Pleasures, plunge themselves in a Pool of lawless Sensuality; so that in order to be happy, they make themselves Beasts, nay worse than they; living in Defiance to all the Dictates of Reason, and of GOD; purchasing at the Price of their eternal Salvation, these poor Pleasures, which being of a gross Nature, limited Degree, and contracted Duration, de-

base the Dignity of the Soul, and defile its Honours; but can
neither suit its noble Nature, and perpetual Existence, nor satisfy
its sublime and intense Desires.

But there is yet another Generation, of as mean and sordid
Wretches, in whose grovling Bosoms, beats nothing that is great
or generous; who imagine Happiness is to be had in temporal
Wealth and Riches. *This,* these *Moles* are in the continual and
eager Chase of; to *this Mark* all the Lines of their busy Thoughts,
anxious Cares, subtle Projects, humerous Speeches, strong Desires, and unwearied Labours bend and terminate. But poor
Creatures, if ye did obtain that Measure of Riches ye seek after,
do ye think it would better your State, bound your Wishes, or
secure your Happiness? No! no! don't ye see the contrary with
your Eyes, that the most grow in Wickedness, in Proportion to
the Increase of their Wealth, and that instead of satiating, it
does but whet their Appetite for more; and ye should remember
that the *Redemption of the Soul is precious, and that it ceaseth
for ever.* As to these Things, a high Mountain afar off seems
to touch the Clouds, but when we come near, the Distance seems
as great as before. Not to add, that temporal Enjoyments are of
very uncertain Continuance. *Why then do ye spend your Money
for that which is not Bread, and your Labours for that which
satisfies not?* . . . O! that I could persuade you, dears Sirs, to
seek with restless and persevering Importunity, an Interest in
those unsearchable Riches; without them ye cannot be rich, in
any valuable Respect, and with them ye cannot be poor.

I wou'd direct my Exhortation to graceless Persons, in various
Conditions of Life.

Are ye poor in Temporals, and do ye find but little Rest and
Comfort in this World? Oh! then will ye be persuaded to accept
of the most durable and noble *Riches, Riches* most dearly purchased, by no less a Price than the Blood of GOD; *Riches* most
freely, frequently, and condescendingly offered, by the Love of
GOD in the Ministry of his Servants, upon the most easy and most
honourable Terms, that the Majesty and Purity of the divine
Nature, and the Dignity and Felicity of the human Nature could
admit. Poor Sinners, you are under peculiar Obligations to seek
for and accept of the Riches of Grace and Glory, least ye be

miserable in both Worlds. It is a most dreadful and shocking Consideration, to think that ye should make a hard Shift, to rub through the many Difficulties, Labours, and Sorrows of this present World, to enter into ten thousand Times worse in the next. Where there will be no *Hope*, no *Ease*, no *Interruption*, no *End*. Alas, my Brethren! It had been better for you ye had never been born, than that this should be your *dismal, dismal* Lot. Others have some sorry sensual Comfort in this Life, but ye have none, or next to none. Oh! it is most terrible to think, to be without Comfort and Quiet in both Worlds! Dear Sirs! If ye had but the Riches of a SAVIOUR's Love, it wou'd sweeten your present Difficulties, conform you to the suffering REDEEMER, support your sorrowful Souls, with the certain Prospect of perfect Felicity, and distinguished Glory, in the next State. For as the Apostle observes, with a noble Emphasis, 2 Cor. iv. 17. *Our light Affliction, which is but for a Moment, worketh for us a far more exceeding, and eternal Weight of Glory.*

O unhappy Sinners! It would not be hard to persuade you, I suppose, to accept of worldly Riches, and why then will ye not be induc'd to accept of Riches worth Millions of Worlds? Sirs, here, in the blessed Gospel, is the glorious *Pearl* of Price, the inestimable *Jewels* of the Covenant, try'd *Gold*, more pure and noble than that of *Ophir, Peru,* and *Mexico;* and white *Raiment*, to enrich and adorn you; and will ye not accept them, on the reasonable Terms they are offered? O cruel Murder! O vile Ingratitude! O detestable Madness! Be astonished and horribly afraid ye Heavens and Earth at this! Ah ye blessed Angels; ye cannot but wonder to see this terrible Tragedy acted! O ye Saints of GOD! look how the adorable dying SAVIOUR, and the rich Purchase of his Blood, is slighted by indigent, ungrateful, and degenerous Rebels! Oh! Can ye keep your Hearts from Mourning on this Account? See what huge Numbers of Mankind are lying in their Blood and Gore, and yet wont accept of Help and Healing, when it is freely offered. If ye can keep your Hearts from Bleeding upon this Occasion, they are very hard indeed! Ah! It pierces my very Soul, to see my Lord and the Riches of his bleeding Love, treated with such Indifference; while on the contrary, Things of an infinitely meaner Nature, and shorter Duration, are courted and labour'd for with the greatest Vehemence. Truly, Brethren, I know not how to express my Sorrows on this Account; if I could bewail it in Tears of Blood, I would.

Are ye in Bondage and Servitude? here is a spiritual, noble, and everlasting Liberty offered to you, in the Riches of Christ! Oh! if the Son of the Father's Love do but make you free, ye will be free indeed.

Are ye rich in worldly Goods? then I beseech you seriously and speedily to consider, that awful Parable of *Dives* and *Lazarus,* and especially the 23, 24, and 25 Verses of it. *And in Hell he lift up his Eyes being in Torments, and seeth* Abraham *afar off, and* Lazarus *in his Bosom. And he cryed, and said. Father* Abraham *have Mercy on me, and send* Lazarus *that he may dip the Tip of his Finger in Water, and cool my Tongue; for I am tormented in this Flame. But* Abraham *said, Son, remember that thou in thy Life-time receivedst thy good Things, and likewise* Lazarus *evil Things: But now he is comforted, and thou art tormented.* O poor unhappy Sinners! see what a dreadful Change there will be in your Condition in a little Time. Remember ye that now wallow in generous Wines, ye will quickly (except ye repent) want Water to cool your flaming Tongues, but shall not obtain a single Drop; ye will be obliged to make your humble Court to these pious Poor, you now contemn as the Dirt under your Feet.

5   *Jonathan Edwards*
The Surprising Work of God (1736)

Jonathan Edwards (1703–1758) has been called one of the foremost philosophers and theologians of the American continent. But—like his grandfather and predecessor in the Northampton, Massachusetts

SOURCE. Jonathan Edwards, *A Faithful Narrative of the Surprising Work of God, in the Conversion of Many Hundred Souls in Northampton, and the Neighboring Towns. . . . In a Letter to the Rev. Dr. Benjamin Colman of Boston* (Boston: Kneeland and Green, 1737), in *The Works of President Edwards,* New York: Leavitt, Trow & Co., 1844, III, pp. 231–237, 238.

pulpit, Solomon Stoddard—he was an evangelist, ever anxious to
witness and even be the instrument of God's working on the souls of
men. And Edwards' Connecticut valley, like the Delaware Valley of
the Tennents, was marked by recurrent revivals. In 1736, writing to
the Rev. Benjamin Colman of Boston—a letter subsequently revised
and enlarged for publication—Edwards described the course of religion
in Northampton, with particular attention to the revival that broke out
in 1734.

The people of the country in general, I suppose are as sober,
orderly, and good sort of people, as in any part of New England;
and I believe they have been preserved the freest by far, of any
part of the country from error and variety of sects and opinions.
Our being so far within the land, at a distance from seaports,
and in a corner of the country, has doubtless been one reason
why we have not been so much corrupted with vice, as most
other parts. But without question the religion, and good order
of the country, and their purity in doctrine, has, under God,
been very much owing to the great abilities, and eminent piety,
of my venerable and honoured grandfather Stoddard. I suppose
we have been the freest of any part of the land from unhappy
divisions, and quarrels in our ecclesiastical and religious
affairs. . . .

We being much separated from other parts of the province,
and having comparatively but little intercourse with them, have
. . . till now, always managed our ecclesiastical affairs within
ourselves; it is the way in which the country, from its infancy,
has gone on by the practical agreement of all, and the way in
which our peace and good order has hitherto been maintained.

The town of Northampton is of about eighty-two years standing, and has now about two hundred families; which mostly dwell
more compactly together than any town of such a bigness in
these parts of the country; which probably has been an occasion
that both our corruptions and reformations have been, from time
to time, the more swiftly propagated, from one to another
through the town. Take the town in general, and so far as I
can judge they are as rational and understanding a people as

most I have been acquainted with. Many of them have been noted for religion, and particularly, have been remarkable for their distinct knowledge in things that relate to heart religion, and Christian experience, and their great regards thereto.

I am the third minister that has been settled in the town. The Reverend Mr. Eleazer Mather, who was the first, was ordained in July, 1669. He was one whose heart was much in his work, abundant in labors for the good of precious souls; he had the high esteem and great love of his people, and was blessed with no small success. The Rev. Mr. Stoddard who succeeded him, came first to the town the November after his death, but was not ordained till September 11, 1672, and died February 11, 1729. So that he continued in the work of the ministry here from his first coming to town, near sixty years. And as he was eminent and renowned for his gifts and grace, so he was blessed, from the beginning, with extraordinary success in his ministry, in the conversion of many souls. He had *five harvests,* as he called them. The first was about fifty-seven years ago; the second about fifty-three years; the third about forty; the fourth about twenty-four; the fifth and last about eighteen years ago. Some of these times were much more remarkable than others, and the ingathering of souls more plentiful. Those about fifty-three, and forty, and twenty-four years ago, were much greater than either the first or the last. But in each of them, I have heard my grandfather say, the greater part of the young people in the town, seemed to be mainly concerned for their eternal salvation.

After the last of these came a far more degenerate time (at least among the young people), I suppose, than ever before. Mr. Stoddard, indeed, had the comfort before he died, of seeing a time when there was no small appearance of a divine work amongst some, and a considerable ingathering of souls, even after I was settled with him in the ministry, which was about two years before his death; and I have reason to bless God for the great advantage I had by it. In these two years there were near twenty that Mr. Stoddard hoped to be savingly converted; but there was nothing of any general awakening. The greater part seemed to be at that time very insensible of the things of religion, and engaged in other cares and pursuits. Just after my grand-

father's death, it seemed to be a time of extraordinary dullness
in religion. Licentiousness for some years greatly prevailed
among the youth of the town; they were many of them very
much addicted to night walking, and frequenting the tavern, and
lewd practices, wherein some by their example exceedingly corrupted others. It was their manner very frequently to get together
in conventions of both sexes, for mirth and jollity, which they
called frolicks; and they would often spend the greater part of
the night in them, without any regard to order in the families
they belonged to. And indeed family government did too much
fail in the town. It was become very customary with many of
our young people to be indecent in their carriage at meeting,
which doubtless would not have prevailed to such a degree, had
it not been that my grandfather, through his great age (though
he retained his powers surprisingly to the last), was not so able
to observe them. There had also long prevailed in the town a
spirit of contention between two parties, into which they had
for many years been divided, by which was maintained a jealousy one of the other, and they were prepared to oppose one
another in all public affairs.

But in two or three years after Mr. Stoddard's death, there
began to be a sensible amendment of these evils. The young
people showed more of a disposition to hearken to counsel, and
by degrees left off their frolicking, and grew observably more
decent in their attendance on the public worship, and there were
more that manifested a religious concern than there used to be.

At the latter end of the year 1733, there appeared a very
unusual flexibleness, and yielding to advice, in our young people.
It had been too long their manner to make the evening after
the Sabbath, and after our public lecture, to be especially the
times of their mirth, and company keeping. But a sermon was
now preached on the Sabbath before the lecture, to show the
evil tendency of the practice, and to persuade them to reform it;
and it was urged on heads of families, that it should be a thing
agreed upon among them, to govern their families, and keep
their children at home, at these times. . . . It was more privately moved, that they should meet together the next day, in
their several neighborhoods, to know each other's minds. Which
was accordingly done, and the motion complied with throughout

the town. But parents found little or no occasion for the exercise of government in the case; the young people declared themselves convinced by what they had heard from the pulpit, and were willing of themselves to comply with the counsel that had been given. And it was immediately, and, I suppose, almost universally complied with, and there was a thorough reformation of these disorders thenceforward, which has continued ever since.

Presently after this, there began to appear a remarkable religious concern at a little village belonging to the congregation, called Pascommuck, where a few families were settled, at about three miles distance from the main body of the town. At this place a number of persons seemed to be savingly wrought upon. In the April following, anno 1734, there happened a very sudden and awful death of a young man in the bloom of his youth; who being violently seized with a pleurisy, and taken immediately very delirious, died in about two days; which (together with what was preached publicly on that occasion) much affected many young people. This was followed with another death of a young married woman, who had been considerably exercised in mind, about the salvation of her soul, before she was ill, and was in great distress, in the beginning of her illness, but seemed to have satisfying evidences of God's saving mercy to her, before her death, so that she died very full of comfort, in a most earnest and moving manner, warning and counselling others. This seemed much to contribute to the solemnizing of the spirits of many young persons, and there began evidently to appear more of a religious concern on people's minds.

In the fall of the year, I proposed it to the young people, that they should agree among themselves to spend the evenings after lectures, in social religion, and to that end divide themselves into several companies to meet in various parts of the town; which was accordingly done, and those meetings have been since continued, and the example imitated by elder people. This was followed with the death of an elderly person, which was attended with many unusual circumstances, by which many were much moved and affected.

About this time began the great noise that was in this part of the country, about Arminianism, which seemed to appear with a very threatening aspect upon the interest of religion here.

The friends of vital piety trembled for fear of the issue. But it seemed, contrary to their fear, strongly to be overruled for the promoting of religion. Many who looked on themselves as in a Christless condition seemed to be awakened by it, with fear that God was about to withdraw from the land, and that we should be given up to heterodoxy, and corrupt principles, and that then their opportunity for obtaining salvation would be past. And many who were brought a little to doubt about the truth of the doctrines they had hitherto been taught, seemed to have a kind of a trembling fear with their doubts, lest they should be led into by-paths, to their eternal undoing. And they seemed with much concern and engagedness of mind to inquire what was indeed the way in which they must come to be accepted with God. There were some things said publicly on that occasion, concerning justification by faith alone.

Although great fault was found with meddling with the controversy in the pulpit, by such a person, and at that time, and though it was ridiculed by many elsewhere, yet it proved a word spoken in season here, and was most evidently attended with a very remarkable blessing of heaven to the souls of the people in this town. They received thence a general satisfaction, with respect to the main thing in question, which they had in trembling doubts and concern about, and their minds were engaged the more earnestly to seek that they might come to be accepted of God, and saved in the way of the gospel, which had been made evident to them to be the true and only way. And then it was, in the latter part of December, that the Spirit of God began extraordinarily to set in, and wonderfully to work amongst us. And there were, very suddenly, one after another, five or six persons, who were, to all appearance, savingly converted, and some of them wrought upon in a very remarkable manner.

Particularly, I was surprised with the relation of a young woman, who had been one of the greatest company keepers in the whole town. When she came to me, I had never heard that she was become in any wise serious, but by the conversation I then had with her, it appeared to me, that what she gave an account of, was a glorious work of God's infinite power and sovereign grace, and that God had given her a new heart, truly broken and sanctified. I could not then doubt of it, and have seen much in my acquaintance with her since to confirm it.

Though the work was glorious, yet I was filled with concern about the effect it might have upon others. I was ready to conclude (though too rashly) that some would be hardened by it, in carelessness and looseness of life, and would take occasion from it to open their mouths in reproaches of religion. But the event was the reverse, to a wonderful degree. God made it, I suppose, the greatest occasion of awakening to others, of any thing that ever came to pass in the town. I have had abundant opportunity to know the effect it had, by my private conversation with many. The news of it seemed to be almost like a flash of lightning, upon the hearts of young people, all over the town, and upon many others. Those persons amongst us, who used to be farthest from seriousness, and that I most feared would make an ill improvement of it, seemed greatly to be awakened with it. Many went to talk with her, concerning what she had met with, and what appeared in her seemed to be to the satisfaction of all that did so.

Presently upon this, a great and earnest concern about the great things of religion, and the eternal world, became universal in all parts of the town, and among persons of all degrees, and all ages. The noise amongst the dry bones waxed louder and louder. All other talk but about spiritual and eternal things was soon thrown by. All the conversation in all companies, and upon all occasions, was upon these things only, unless so much as was necessary for people carrying on their ordinary secular business. Other discourse than of the things of religion, would scarcely be tolerated in any company. The minds of people were wonderfully taken off from the world; it was treated amongst us as a thing of very little consequence. They seemed to follow their worldly business, more as a part of their duty, than from any disposition they had to it. The temptation now seemed to lie on that hand, to neglect worldly affairs too much, and to spend too much time in the immediate exercise of religion. Which thing was exceedingly misrepresented by reports that were spread in distant parts of the land, as though the people here had wholly thrown by all worldly business, and betook themselves entirely to reading and praying, and such like religious exercises.

But though the people did not ordinarily neglect their worldly business . . . religion was with all sorts the great concern, and the world was a thing only by the by. The only thing in their view was to get the kingdom of heaven, and every one appeared pressing into it. The engagedness of their hearts in this great concern could not be hid. It appeared in their very countenances. It then was a dreadful thing amongst us to lie out of Christ, in danger every day of dropping into hell, and what persons minds were intent upon was to escape for their lives, and to *fly from the wrath to come.* All would eagerly lay hold of opportunities for their souls, and were wont very often to meet together in private houses, for religious purposes. And such meetings, when appointed, were wont greatly to be thronged.

There was scarcely a single person in the town, either old or young, that was left unconcerned about the great things of the eternal world. Those that were wont to be the vainest, and loosest, and those that had been most disposed to think and speak slightly of vital and experimental religion, were now generally subject to great awakenings. And the work of conversion was carried on in a most astonishing manner, and increased more and more. Souls did, as it were, come by flocks to Jesus Christ. From day to day, for many months together, might be seen evident instances of sinners brought *out of darkness into marvellous light,* and delivered *out of an horrible pit, and from the miry clay, and set upon a rock* with *a new song of praise to God in their mouths.*

This work of God, as it was carried on, and the number of true saints multiplied, soon made a glorious alteration in the town; so that in the spring and summer following, anno 1735, the town seemed to be full of the presence of God. It never was so full of love, nor so full of joy, and yet so full of distress as it was then. There were remarkable tokens of God's presence in almost every house. It was a time of joy in families on the account of salvation's being brought unto them; parents rejoicing over their children as new born, and husbands over their wives, and wives over their husbands. *The goings of God were then seen in his sanctuary, God's day was a delight, and his tabernacles were amiable.* Our public assemblies were then beautiful. The congregation was alive in God's service, every one earnestly intent on the public worship, every hearer eager to drink in the words of the minister as they came from his mouth. The assembly in general were, from time to time, in tears while the word was preached, some weeping with sorrow and distress, others with joy and love, others with pity and concern for the souls of their neighbors. . . .

When this work of God first appeared, and was so extraordinarily carried on amongst us in the winter, others round about us seemed not to know what to make of it. And there were many that scoffed at, and ridiculed it; and some compared what we called conversion to certain distempers. But it was very observable of many, that occasionally came amongst us from abroad, with disregardful hearts, that what they saw here cured them of such a temper of mind. Strangers were generally surprised to find things so much beyond what they had heard, and were wont to tell others that the state of the town could not be conceived of by those who had not seen it. The notice that was taken of it by the people that came to town on occasion of the court, that sat here in the beginning of March, was very observable. And those that came from the neighborhood to our public lectures, were for the most part remarkably affected. Many that came to town, on one occasion or other, had their consciences smitten, and awakened, and went home with wounded hearts, and with those impressions that never wore off till they had hopefully a saving issue. And those that before had serious thoughts, had their awakenings and convictions greatly increased. And there were many instances of persons that came from abroad, on visits, or on business, that had not been long here before, to all appearance, they were savingly wrought upon, and partook of that shower of divine blessing that God rained down here, and went home rejoicing; till at length the same work began evidently to appear and prevail in several other towns in the country. . . .

But this shower of divine blessing has been yet more extensive: there was no small degree of it in some parts of the Jerseys, as I was informed when I was at New-York (in a long journey I took at that time of the year for my health), by some people of the Jerseys, whom I saw. Especially the Reverend Mr. William Tennent, a minister, who seemed to have such things much at heart, told me of a very great awakening of many in a place called the Mountains, under the ministry of one Mr. Cross, and of a very considerable revival of religion in another place under the ministry of his brother the Rev. Mr. Gilbert Tennent, and also at another place, under the ministry of a very pious young gentleman, a Dutch minister, whose name as I remember was Freelinghousen.

This seems to have been a very extraordinary dispensation of Providence. God has in many respects, gone out of, and much beyond his usual and ordinary way.

THE GREAT ITINERANT

6   *In Philadelphia (1739)*

Into this scene stepped George Whitefield (1714–1770), and it was Whitefield who served to crystallize the here-and-there awakenings into a continent-wide revival. Emerging from the Wesleyan movement of England, he visited Georgia for a few months in 1738, returned briefly to England, and then arrived in Philadelphia in December 1739. From there he made trips into the South and through New England, in seventy–three days in 1740 traveling eight hundred miles and preaching one hundred and thirty sermons. Advertisements and pamphlets preceded his "progress," ministers of many viewpoints welcomed him at first to their churches, and an awakened populace was left in his wake. In January 1741 he sailed for England, but he was to make five more travels through America during the succeeding three decades—none as vibrant as this first, however. The witty, urbane Benjamin Franklin (1706–1790) describes Whitefield's activities and his effect on Philadelphia.

In 1739 arriv'd among us from England the Rev. Mr. Whitefiel, who had made himself remarkable there as an itinerant Preacher. He was at first permitted to preach in some of our

SOURCE. Leonard W. Labaree, *et al.,* eds., *The Autobiography of Benjamin Franklin,* New Haven and London: Yale University Press, 1964, pp. 175–180. Reprinted by permission of Yale University Press and the University of California Press, whose *Benjamin Franklin's Memoirs Parallel Text Edition,* Max Farrand, ed. (Berkeley, 1949) served as the basic text in the preparation of the Yale edition.

Churches; but the Clergy taking a Dislike to him, soon refus'd him their Pulpits and he was oblig'd to preach in the Fields. The Multitudes of all Sects and Denominations that attended his Sermons were enormous, and it was matter of Speculation to me who was one of the Number, to observe the extraordinary Influence of his Oratory on his Hearers, and how much they admir'd and respected him, notwithstanding his common Abuse of them, by assuring them they were naturally *half Beasts and half Devils.* It was wonderful to see the Change soon made in the Manners of our Inhabitants; from being thoughtless or indifferent about Religion, it seem'd as if all the World were growing Religious; so that one could not walk thro' the Town in an Evening without Hearing Psalms sung in different Families of every Street. And it being found inconvenient to assemble in the open Air, subject to its Inclemencies, the Building of a House to meet in was no sooner propose'd and Persons appointed to receive Contributions, but sufficient Sums were soon receiv'd to procure the Ground and erect the Building which was 100 feet long and 70 broad, about the Size of Westminster-hall; and the Work was carried on with such Spirit as to be finished in a much shorter time than could have been expected. Both House and Ground were vested in Trustees, expressly for the Use of any Preacher of any religious Persuasion who might desire to say something to the People of Philadelphia, the Design in building not being to accommodate any particular Sect, but the Inhabitants in general, so that even if the Mufti of Constantinople were to send a Missionary to preach Mahometanism to us, he would find a Pulpit at his Service. (The Contributions being made by People of different Sects promiscuously, Care was taken in the Nomination of Trustees to avoid giving a Predominancy to any Sect, so that one of each was appointed, viz. one Church of England-man, one Presbyterian, one Baptist, one Moravian, &c.).

Mr. Whitfield, in leaving us, went preaching all the Way thro' the Colonies to Georgia. The Settlement of that Province had lately been begun; but instead of being made with hardy industrious Husbandmen accustomed to Labour, the only People fit for such an Enterprise, it was with Families of broken Shopkeepers and other insolvent Debtors, many of indolent and idle habits, taken out of the Gaols, who being set down in the Woods, unqualified for clearing Land, and unable to endure the Hardships of a new Settlement, perished in Numbers, leaving many helpless Children unprovided for. The Sight of their miserable Situation inspired the benevolent Heart of Mr. Whitefield with the Idea of building an Orphan House there, in which they might be supported and educated. Returning northward he preach'd up this Charity, and made large Collections; for his Eloquence had a wonderful Power over the Hearts and Purses of his Hearers, of which I myself was an Instance. I did not disapprove of the Design, but as Georgia was then destitute of Materials and Workmen, and it was propos'd to send them from Philadelphia at a great Expence, I though it would have been better to have built the House here and brought the Children to it. This I advis'd, but he was resolute in his first Project, and rejected my Counsel, and I thereupon refus'd to contribute. I happened soon after to attend one of his Sermons, in the Course of which I perceived he intended to finish with a Collection, and I silently resolved he should get nothing from me. I had in my Pocket a Handful of Copper Money, three or four silver Dollars, and five Pistoles in Gold. As he proceeded I began to soften, and concluded to give the Coppers. Another Stroke of his Oratory made me asham'd of that, and determin'd me to give the Silver; and he finish'd so admirably, that I empty'd my Pocket wholly into the Collector's Dish, Gold and all. . . .

Some of Mr. Whitfield's Enemies affected to suppose that he would apply these Collections to his own private Emolument; but I, who was intimately acquainted with him, (being employ'd in printing his Sermons and Journals, &c.) never had the least Suspicion of his Integrity, but am to this day decidedly of Opinion that he was in all his Conduct, a perfectly *honest Man*. And methinks my Testimony in his Favour ought to have the more Weight, as we had no religious Connection. He us'd indeed sometimes to pray for my Conversion, but never had the Satisfaction of believing that his Prayers were heard. Ours were a mere civil Friendship, sincere on both Sides, and lasted to his Death.

The following Instance will show something of the Terms on which we stood. Upon one of his Arrivals from England at Boston, he wrote to me that he should come soon to Philadelphia, but knew not where he could lodge when there, as he understood his old kind Host Mr. Benezet was remov'd to Germantown. My Answer was; You know my House, if you can make shift with its scanty Accommodations you will be most heartily welcome. He reply'd, that if I made that kind Offer for Christ's sake, I should not miss of a Reward. And I return'd, *Don't let me be mistaken; it was not for Christ's sake, but for your sake.* One of our common Acquaintance jocosely remark'd, that knowing it to be the Custom of the Saints, when they receiv'd any favour, to shift the Burthen of the Obligation from off their own Shoulders, and place it in Heaven, I had contriv'd to fix it on Earth.

The last time I saw Mr. Whitefield was in London, when he consulted me about his Orphan House Concern, and his Purpose of appropriating it to the Establishment of a College.

He had a loud and clear Voice, and articulated his Words and Sentences so perfectly that he might be heard and understood at a great Distance, especially as his Auditories, however numerous, observ'd the most exact Silence. He preach'd one Evening from the Top of the Court House Steps, which are in the Middle of Market Street, and on the West Side of Second Street which crosses it at right angles. Both Streets were fill'd with his Hearers to a considerable Distance. Being among the hindmost in Market Street, I had the Curiosity to learn how far he could be heard, by retiring backwards down the Street towards the River, and I found his Voice distinct till I came near Front-Street, when some Noise in that Street, obscur'd it. Imagining then a Semi-Circle, of which my Distance should be the Radius, and that it were fill'd with Auditors, to each of whom I allow'd two square feet, I computed that he might well be heard by more than Thirty-Thousand. This reconcil'd me to the Newspaper Accounts of his having preach'd to 25000 People in the Fields, and to the antient Histories of Generals haranguing whole Armies, of which I had sometimes doubted.

By hearing him often I came to distinguish easily between Sermons newly compos'd, and those which he had often preach'd in the Course of his Travels. His Delivery of the latter was so improv'd by frequent Repetitions, that every Accent, every Emphasis, every Modulation of Voice, was so perfectly well turn'd and well plac'd, that without being interested in the Subject, one could not help being pleas'd with the Discourse, a Pleasure of much the same kind with that receiv'd from an excellent Piece of Musick. This is an Advantage itinerant Preachers have over those who are stationary: as the latter cannot well improve their Delivery of a Sermon by so many Rehearsals.

His Writing and Printing from time to time gave great Advantage to his Enemies. Unguarded Expressions and even erroneous Opinions del [ivere] d in Preaching might have been afterwards explain'd, or qualify'd by supposing others that might have accompany'd them; or they might have been deny'd; But *litera scripta manet* [The written letter remains]. Critics attack'd his Writings violently, and with so much Appearance of Reason as to diminish the Number of his Votaries, and prevent their Encrease. So that I am of Opinion, if he had never written any thing he would have left behind him a much more numerous and important Sect. And his Reputation might in that case have been still growing, even after his Death; as there being nothing of his Writing on which to found a censure; and give him a lower Character, his Proselites would be left at liberty to feign for him as great a Variety of Excellencies, as their enthusiastic Admiration might wish him to have possessed.

7 *In Charleston (1740)*

Whitefield's own Journal, which he wrote and published as he went along—an effective piece of "self-advertising"—best gives the itinerary of his wandering ministry and the audacity with which he challenged established churchmen. What follows describes his ministry in Charleston, South Carolina in mid-March 1740, and his confrontation with Alexander Garden, the Bishop of London's Commissary for the colony.

SOURCE. *A Continuation of the Reverend Mr. Whitefield's Journal. From a Few Days After His Arrival in Georgia to His Second Return Thither from Pennsylvania,* Philadelphia: B. Franklin, 1740, pp. 14–21.

Friday, March 14. Arrived last night at *Charleston,* being called there to see my Brother, who lately came from *England,* and had brought me a Packet of Letters from my dear Friends. . . . Waited on the Commissary, with my Brother and other Companions, but met with a cool Reception. After I had been there a little while, I told him that I was inform'd, he had some Questions to propose to me, and that I was now come to give him all the Satisfaction I could in answering them. Upon this I immediately perceived Passion begin to arise in his Heart. "Yes, Sir," says he, "I have several Questions to put to you. But," added he "you have got above us," or something to that Purpose. Then he charged me with *Enthusiasm* and Pride, for speaking against the Generality of the Clergy, and desired I would make my Charge good. I told him, I thought I had already; but, as yet, I had scarce begun with them. He then asked me, Wherein were the Clergy so much to blame? I answered, they did not preach up *Justification by Faith alone;* and, upon talking with the Commissary, I found he was as ignorant of it as any of the rest. He then sneered me, with telling me of my Modesty, expressed in my Letter to the Bishop of *Gloucester.* He charged me with breaking the Canons and Ordination vow; And notwithstanding I told him I was ordained by Letters Dismissory from the Bishop of *London.* Yet in a great rage he told me, if I preached in any publick church in that Province, he would suspend me. I replied, "I shall regard that as much as I would a Pope's Bull. But, Sir," says I, "why should you be offended at my speaking against the Generality of the Clergy, for I always spoke worthily of you?". . . I further added, "Sir, you did not behave thus, when I was with you last." "No," says he, "you did not speak against the Clergy," or some such thing. "Because," replied I, "more light has been given me since that time. But if you will make an application to yourself, be pleased, Sir, to let me ask you one Question: have you delivered your Soul by exclaiming against the Assemblies and Balls here?" "What, Sir," says he, "must you come to catechise me? No, I have not exclaim'd against them; I think there is no Harm in them." "Then, Sir," said I, "I shall think it my Duty to exclaim against you." "Then, Sir," replied he, *(in a very great Rage)* "get you out of my House." Upon which I made my Bow, and, with my

Friends took my leave, pitying the Commissary, who I really tho't was more noble than to give such Treatment. After this, we went to publick prayers, dined at a Friend's House, drank Tea with the *Independent* Minister, and preached about four in the Afternoon, to a large Auditory in his Meeting-House. . . .

Saturday, March 15. Breakfasted, sung a Hymn, and had some religious Conversation on board my Brother's Ship. Preached in the *Baptist* Meeting-House, and was much pleased, when I heard afterwards, that from the same Pulpit, a Person not long ago, had preached, who denied the Doctrine of Original Sin, the Divinity and Righteousness of our dear Lord, and the Operations of God's blessed Spirit upon the Heart. I was led out to shew the utter Inability of Man to save himself, and the absolute Necessity of his depending on the rich and sovereign Grace of God in Christ Jesus, in order to be restored to his primitive Dignity. Some, I observ'd, were put under concern, and most seem'd willing to know, whether those Things were so. In the Evening I preach'd again in the *Independent* Meeting-House, to a more attentive Auditory than ever; And had the Pleasure afterwards of Finding that a Gentlewoman, whose Family has been carried away for some time with Deistical Principles, began now to be unhinged, and to see that there was no Rest in such a Scheme, for a fallen Creature to rely on. Lord Jesus, *for thy Mercy's Sake, reveal thyself in her Heart, and make her willing to know the Truth as it is in thee.* Amen, *and* Amen.

Sunday, March 16. Preached at Eight in the Morning at the Scotch Meeting-House, to a large Congregation; visited a sick person; went to Church; heard the Commissary represent me under the Character of the *Pharisee,* who came to the Temple, saying, "God, *I thank thee that I am not as other Men are."* But whether I do what I do out of a Principle of Pride, or Duty, the Searcher of Hearts will discover 'ere long, before Men and Angels. Found myself very sick and weak at Dinner. Went to church again, and preached about Five, in the *Independent* Meeting-House Yard, the House itself not being near capacious enough to hold the Auditory. . . .

Felt much Freedom after Sermon in talking to a large Company at a Merchant's House, and then supped with another Friend. Expounded Part of the Chapter, prayed and went to our Lodgings with my dear Companions, praising and blessing God. *Hasten that Time, O Lord, when we shall join the Heavenly Choir that is now about Thy Throne.*

Monday, March 17. Preach'd in the Morning at the *Independent* Meeting-House, and was more explicit than ever, in exclaiming against Balls and Assemblies, to which the People seem'd to hearken with much Attention.

Preached again in the Evening, and being excited thereto by some of the Inhabitants, spoke on Behalf of my poor Orphans. God was pleased to give it his Blessing, and I collected upwards of *Seventy Pounds Sterling* for them, the largest Collection I ever yet made on that Occasion. A further Earnest to me, that we shall yet see great things in *America,* and that God will carry on and finish the Work, begun in his Name at *Georgia.*

Tuesday, March 18. Preached twice again today, and took an affectionate Leave of, and gave Thanks to, my Hearers for their great Liberality. Many wept, and my own Heart yearn'd much towards them. For I believe a good Work is begun in many Souls. Generally every Day several came to me, telling me with weeping Eyes, how God had been pleas'd to convince them, by the Word preach'd, and how desirous they were of laying hold on, and having an Interest in the compleat and everlasting Righteousness of the Lord Jesus Christ. Numbers desired privately to converse with me. Many sent me little presents as Tokens of their Love, and earnestly entreated that I would come mongst them again. Invitations were given me from some of the adjacent Villages, and People daily came to Town more and more from their Plantations to hear the Word. . . . The Congregations grew larger on the Week Days, and many Things concurred to induce us to think that God intended to visit some in *Charlestown* with his Salvation.

8   *In Middletown, Connecticut (1740)*

But it is not in Whitefield, or even Franklin, that we sense the pro-
found impression that "the great itinerant" made on the throngs who
heard him preach. Of his sermon at Middletown, Connecticut on Oc-
tober 23, 1740, for example, Whitefield simply recorded: "Preached to
about 4,000 people (great Numbers of which were considerably affected)
about 11 o'Clock." Nathan Cole, farmer and carpenter of Kensington
Parish, a dozen miles from Middletown, a man who, before hearing
Whitefield, "intended to be saved by my own works such as prayers
and good deeds" (reflecting the "arminianism" of those ministers
criticized for long by the Stoddards, Wigglesworths, and Edwardses of
New England) tells us much more in the crude journal of his "Spiritual
Travels": the almost breathless anticipation of Whitefield's coming,
the haste and fear that the sermon would be missed, and the even
greater fear of wrathful Jehovah that Whitefield provoked.

Now it pleased God to send Mr. Whitfeld into this land, and
my hearing of his preaching at Philadelphia like one of the old
aposels, and [of] many thousands flocking after him to hear the
gospel, and great numbers. . . converted to Christ, I felt the
spirit of God drawing me by conviction. I longed to see and
hear him and wished he would come this way. And I soon
heard he was come to New York and the Jerseys, and [of] great
multitudes flocking after him under great concern for their Soule,
and many converted, wich brought on my concern more and
more, hoping soon to see him. But next I herd he was on Long
Iland, and next at Boston, and next at Northampton. And then
one morning, all on a Suding about 8 or 9 o Clock, there came
a messenger and said Mr. Whitfeld preached at Hartford and

SOURCE. "The Spiritual Travels of Nathan Cole," extracted in George
Leon Walker, *Some Aspects of the Religious Life of New England, with*
special reference to Congregationalists (Boston & New York: Silver, Burdett
and Co., 1897) , pp. 89–92.

Weathersfield yesterday and is to preach at Middeltown this morning at 10 o clock. I was in my field at work [and] I dropt my tool that I had in my hand and run home and run thru my house and bade my wife get ready quick to goo and hear Mr. Whitfeld preach at Middeltown. And [I] run to my pasture for my hors with all my might, fearing I should be too late to hear him. I brought my hors home and soon mounted and took my wife up and went forward as fast as I thought the hors could bear, and when my hors began to be out of breath I would get down and put my wife on the Saddel, and bid her ride as fast as she could, and not Stop or Slak for except I bade her. And so I would run untill I was almost out of breth, and then mount my hors again, and so I did severel times to favour my hors. We improved every moment to get along as if we was fleeing for our lives, all this while fearing we should be too late to hear the Sarmon, for we had twelve miles to ride double in littel more than an hour.

And we went round by the upper housen parish, and when we came within about half a mile of the road that comes down from Hartford, Weathersfield and Stepney to Middeltown, on high land, I saw before me a Cloud or fog, rising—I first thought—off from the great river. But as I came nearer the road I heard a noise, something like a low rumbling thunder, and I presently found it was the rumbling of horses feet coming down the road and this Cloud was a Cloud of dust made by the running of horses feet. It arose some rods into the air over the tops of the hills and trees. And when I came within about twenty rods of the road, I could see men and horses Slipping along in the Cloud like shadows. And when I came nearer it was like a stedy streem of horses and their riders, scarcely a horse more then his length behind another, all of a lather and fome with swet, ther breth rooling out of their noistrels. . . . Every hors semed to go with all his might to carry his rider to hear the news from heaven for the saving of their Souls. It made me trembel to see the Sight—how the world was in a strugle!

I found a vacance between two horses to slip in my hors, and my wife said, "Law, our cloaths will be all spoiled. See how they look?" for they was so covered with dust that they looked allmost all of a color, coats and hats and shirts and horses.

We went down in the Streeme. I herd no man speak a word all the way, three mile, but evry one presing forward in great haste. And when we gat down to the old meating house, thare was a great multitude. It was said to be 3 or 4000 of people assembled together.

We gat of from our horses and shook off the dust, and the ministers was then coming to the meating house. I turned and looked toward the great river and saw the fery boats running swift forward and backward, bringing over loads of people. The ores rowed nimble and quick. Everything—men, horses and boats—all seamed to be struglin for life. The land and the banks over the river looked black with people and horses all along the 12 miles. I see no man at work in his field, but all seamed to be gone.

When I see Mr. Whitfeld come upon the Scaffold, he looked almost angellical—a young, slim, slender youth before some thousands of people, and with a bold, undaunted countenance. And my hearing how God was with him everywhere as he came along, it solomnized my mind, and put me in a trembling fear before he began to preach, for he looked as if he was Cloathed with authority from the great God. And a sweet, solomn Solemnity sat upon his brow, and my hearing him preach gave me a heart wound, by god's blessing. My old foundation was broken up and I saw that my righteousness would not save me. Then I was convinced of the doctrine of Election, and went right to quareling with God about it, because all that I could do would not save me, and he had decreed from Eternity who should be saved and who not. I began to think I was not Elected, and that God made some for heaven and me for hell. And I thought God was not Just in so doing. I thought I did not stand on even Ground with others if, as I thought, I was made to be damned. My heart then rose against God exceedingly for his making me for hell. [And] this distress lasted almost two years.

9 In Virginia

Whitefield's influence was felt in Virginia, too. There a zealous indigenous dissent from the established church had grown up, particularly in Hanover County. But the movement took form as its leading figures read Whitefield's sermons and as Presbyterian itinerants came south from the Delaware Valley. Finally, in 1747, Samuel Davies (1723–1761) arrived. A strenuous preacher—he was soon ministering regularly to seven congregations in five counties and traveling throughout the colony to organize revival meetings—Davies was even more important in bringing orderly Presbyterianism to the colony and obtaining recognition from the Virginia government. In 1751, in a pamphlet published in Boston, he described the origins of the Virginia movement.

The Few that profess'd a Dissatisfaction with the general Strain of Preaching in Church, and therefore either absented themselves, or attended with Murmuring and Reluctance, were generally counted whimsical Creatures, and hypocritical Affectors of Singularity. And indeed they could not but own their Sentiments singular, for they knew of none in the present Age of the same Mind with them and therefore had no Prospect of obtaining a Minister to preach to them those Doctrines they thirsted for. Their Notions, as far as I can learn, were found in the main (tho' intermix'd with some corrupt Notions verging towards *Antinomianism)* the opposite Extreme to that they had left. And tho' this rendered them more odious to their Adversaries and furnished them with Occasions more plausibly to expose them. Yet, considering their Circumstances as being destitute of a judicious Minister to instruct them in the Doctrines of the Gospel, and caution them against Mistakes—and as labouring under the Prejudices of Education and transported with the Sallies of their first Zeal, which is generally imprudent and wild—I am

SOURCE. Samuel Davies, *The State of Religion Among the Protestant Dissenters in Virginia,* Boston: S. Kneeland, 1751, pp. 8–15, 18.

more surprized at their Soundness and Regularity in most Things, than at their Mistakes and Extravagancies in a few.

In this Case about ten or twelve Persons, who are now Members of my Congregation, had been for some Time before the Revival of Religion which began in the Year 1743. One Mr. *Samuel Morris* (for I am not ashamed publickly to mention his Name, notwithstanding the Calumnies flung upon it by many) a Person of a forward, sociable Spirit, who had for some Time been extremely anxious about his eternal State, & unweariedly seeking Relief by all Means within his Reach, at length obtain'd a Discovery of that glorious Method of Salvation thro' Jesus Christ, to which Sinners *from all the Ends of the Earth look, and are saved,* and where they universally agree to fix all their Hopes, notwithstanding the great Diversity of their Circumstances as to Situation, Education, outward Instruction, &c. The distinct Relation he has given me of his Exercises at that Time and since, and the prevailing Piety of his common Behaviour, leave me no Room to be anxious about the Sincerity of his Religion; tho', as it is common in such Cases, his former pious Zeal to do Good, with a few very pardonable Imprudences that attended it, have fix'd an indelible *Odium* on his Character among many who opposed the religious Concern he attempted to promote. After this Discovery of the Gospel, his Soul was anxious for the Salvation of his Neighbours, and inflamed with Zeal to use Means to awaken them. This was the Tendency of his Conversation, and he also read to them such Authors as had been most useful to him, particularly *Luther's Comment upon the Galatians,* which first opened to him the Way of Justification thro' Christ alone, and his *Table-Discourses,* sundry Pieces of honest *Bunyan's* &c. By those Means a few of his Neighbours were made more tho'tful about Religion than usual, and doubtful they had lived 'till then in a careless Ignorance of it. But the Concern was not very extensive.

I have prevailed, Sir, on my good Friend before mentioned, who was the principal private Instrument of promoting the late Work, and therefore well acquainted with it, to write me a Narrative of its Rise & Progress from this Period 'till my Settlement here: and this, together with the Substance of what he and others have told me, I shall present to you without any material Alterations, and personate him, tho' I shall not exactly use his Words.

"The Reverend Mr. *Whitfield* had been in *Virginia*, I think, in the Year 1740, and at the Invitation of the Rev. Mr. *Blair*, our late Commissary, had preached in *Williamsburg*, our Metropolis, about 60 miles from *Hanover*. His Fame was much spread abroad, as a very warm and alarming Preacher, which made such of us in *Hanover* as had been awakened, very eager to see & hear him. But as he left the Colony before we heard of him, we had no Opportunity. But in the Year —43, a young Gentleman arrived from Scotland with a Book of his Sermons preached in *Glasgow*, & taken from his Mouth in short Hand, which with Difficulty I procured. After I had read it with great Liking & Benefit, I invited my Neighbours to come & hear it; and the Plainness, Popularity, & Fervency of the Discourses, being peculiarly fitted to affect our unimproved Minds, and the Lord rendring the Word efficacious, many were convinced of their undone Condition, and constrained to seek deliverance with the greatest Solicitude. A considerable Number convened every Sabbath to hear these Sermons, instead of going to Church, and frequently on Week Days. The Concern of some was so passionate and violent, that they could not avoid crying out, weeping bitterly, &c. and that when such Indications of religious Concern were so strange and ridiculous, that they could not be occasioned by Example or Sympathy, and the Affectation of them would have been so unprofitable an Instance of Hypocrisy, that none could be tempted to it. My Dwelling-House at length was too small to contain the People; whereupon we determined to build a Meeting-House, meerly for Reading; for we knew of no Minister in the World whom we could get to preach to us according to our Liking; and having never been accustomed to social *extempore* Prayer, none of us durst attempt it in Company. By this single Mean sundry were solemnly awakened, and their Conduct ever since is a living Attestation of the Continuance and happy Issue of their Impressions. When the Report of these Sermons and the Effects occasioned by reading them was spread Abroad, I was invited to several Places to read them, at a considerable Distance; and by this Means the Concern was propagated.

"About this Time, our absenting our selves from Church, contrary, as was alledged, to the Laws of the Land, was taken Notice of, and we were called upon by the Court to assign our Reasons for it, and to declare what Denomination we were of. As we knew but little of any Denomination of Dissenters, except *Quakers*, we were at a Loss what Name to assume. At length recollecting that *Luther* was a noted Reformer, and that his Doctrines were agreable to our Sentiments, and had been of special Service to us, we declared our selves *Lutherans*. And thus we continued till Providence afforded us an unexpected Opportunity of hearing the Rev. Mr. *William Robinson*. . . .

"On the 6th of July —43, Mr. *Robinson* preached his first Sermon to us from *Luk*. 13.3 and continued with us preaching four Days successively. The Congregation was large the first Day, and as the Report of him spread, it vastly encreas'd on the three ensuing. 'Tis hard for the liveliest Imagination to form an Image of the Condition of the Assembly on these glorious Days of the Son of Man. Such of us as had been hungring for the Word before, were lost in an agreable Confusion of various Passions, surprized, astonished, pleased, enraptured! so that we were hardly capable of Self-Government, and some could not refrain from publickly declaring their Transport. We were overwhelmed with the Tho'ts of the unexpected Goodness of God, in allowing us to hear the Gospel preached in a Manner that surpassed even our former Wishes, and much more our Hopes. Many that came thro' Curiosity were *pricked to the Heart,* and but few in the numerous Assemblies on these four Days appeared unaffected. They returned astonished, alarmed with Apprehensions of their dangerous Condition, convinced of their former entire ignorance of Religion, and anxiously enquiring what they should do to be saved. And there is Reason to believe there was as much Good done by these four Sermons, as by all the Sermons preached in these Parts before or since.

"Before Mr. *Robinson* left us, he successfully endeavoured to correct some of our *Antinomian* Mistakes, and to bring us to carry on the Worship of God more regularly at our Meetings. He advised us to meet to read good Sermons, and to begin &

conclude with Prayer and singing of Psalms, which 'till then we had omitted. When we met next, we complied with his Directions; and when all the rest refused, I read and prayed with Trembling and Diffidence. Which Method was observed in sundry Places 'till we were furnished with a Minister. The Blessing of God remarkably attended these more private Means, and it was really astonishing to observe the solemn Impressions begun or continued in many by hearing good Discourses read. I had repeated invitations to come to many Places round, some of them 30 or 40 Miles distant, to read, with which I generally comply'd. Considerable Numbers were won't to attend, with eager Attention and awful Solemnity. And sundry were, in a Judgment of Charity, Thoro'ly turned to God, and thereupon erected Meeting-Houses, and chose Readers among themselves, by which the Work was more extensively carried on.

"Soon after our Father, Mr. *Robinson,* left us, the Rev. Mr. *John Blair* paid us a short visit; and truly he came to us *in the Fulness of the Gospel of Christ.* Former Impressions were ripened and new formed on many Hearts. One Night in particular a whole House-full of People was quite over-come with the Power of the Word, particularly of one pungent Sentence that dropt from his Lips. And they could hardly sit or stand, or keep their Passions under any proper Restraints, so general was the Concern during his Stay with us. . . .

"Some Time after this, the Rev. Mr. *John Roan,* was sent by the Presbytery of *New-Castle,* (under whose immediate Care we had voluntarily placed ourselves to supply us.) He continued with us longer than either of the former; and the happy Effects of his Ministrations are still apparent in many Instances. He preached at sundry Places at the earnest Solicitations of the People, which was the happy Occasion of beginning and promoting the religious Concern, where there were little Appearances of it before. This, together with his speaking pretty freely about the Degeneracy of the Clergy in this Colony, gave a general Alarm, and some Measures were concerted to suppress us. To incense the Indignation of the Government the more, a persidious Wretch deposed, he heard Mr. *Roan* use some blasphemous Expressions in his Sermon, and speak in the most shocking & reproachful Manner of the established Church. An Indictment

was thereupon drawn up against Mr. *Roan*, (tho' by that Time
he had departed the Colony) and some of the People who had
invited him to preach at their Houses were cited to appear before
the General Court (which in this Government consists of the
Governour or Commander in Chief, and His Majesty's Council)
and two of them were fined *twenty Shillings* Sterling, besides
the Costs, which in one of the Cases would have amounted to
near *fifty Pounds,* had the Evidences demanded their Due. While
my Cause was upon Trial, I had Reason to rejoyce that the
Throne of Grace is accessible in *all Places,* and that helpless
Creatures can waft up their Desires *unseen,* to God, in the midst
of a Crowd. Six Evidences were cited to prove the Indictment
against Mr. Roan. But their Depositions were in his Favour. And
as for the Evidence mentioned just now, who accused him of
Blasphemy against God and the Church, when he heard of
Messirs. *G. Tennent's* and *S. Finley's* Arrival he fled, and has not
returned since, so that the Indictment was drop'd. I had Reason
to fear being banished the Colony, and all Circumstances seem'd
to threaten the Extirpation of Religion among the Dissenters in
these Parts. . . .

"[Our] present Pastor, was sent by the Presbytery to supply
us about six Week, in Spring, *Anno* 1747, when our Discourage-
ments from the Government were renewed and multiplied. For
on one Sunday the Governour's Proclamation was set up at our
Meeting-House, '*strictly requiring all Magistrates to suppress &
prohibit, as far as they lawfully could, all itinerant Preachers,
&c.*' which occasion'd us to forbear Reading that Day, 'till we
had Time to deliberate and consult what was expedient to do;
but how joyfully were we surprized before the next Sabbath,
when we unexpectedly heard that Mr. *Davies* was come to
preach so long among us; and especially, that he had qualified
himself according to Law, and obtained the Licensure of four
Meeting-Houses among us, which had never been done before!
Thus when our Hopes were expiring, and our Liberties more precarious than ever, we were suddenly advanced to a more secure
Situation. '*Man's Extremity is the Lord's Opportunity.*' For this
seasonable Instance of the Interprosition of divine Providence, we
desire to offer our grateful Praises; and we importune the
Friends of *Zion* generously to concur in the delightful Employ."

REBUTTAL AND DISSENSION

10   *The Hartford North Association (1741)*

That the revivalistic and non-revivalistic ministers were bound to collide was inherent in the situation. Both claimed to be doing God's work, but by their very nature the revivalists put forth the claim more ardently, and they constantly contrasted their own blessed message with that of the "Pharisee-Shepherds, or unconverted Teachers." (The phrase is Gilbert Tennent's.) The great body of the ministry was forced into a dilemma. The religiosity prompted by the awakeners was to be admired, but the awakeners' attack upon themselves was odious. The dilemma was resolved as the awakeners precipitated a near-hysterical frenzy among laymen. A distinction could then be drawn between God's work (religiosity) and the Devil's (too ardent a religiosity). As one minister wrote of an "awakened" town in the fall of 1741: "A great work . . . but more of the footsteps of Satan than in any place I have yet been in; the zeal of some too furious; they tell of many visions, revelations and many strong impressions upon the imagination . . . Satan is using many artful wiles to put a stop to the work of God." The awakeners who had at first been welcomed by most ministers because of the religiosity they provoked could now be condemned for the Satanic outpouring that followed. Such was the case in Connecticut—where ultimately laws would be passed against itinerants—when fifteen ministers of the North Hartford Association met on August 11, 1741, a mere ten months after the passage of George Whitefield through the colony. Their conclusions were in the form of a series of questions and answers.

SOURCE. Records of the Hartford North Association for August 11, 1741, quoted in George Leon Walker, *History of the First Church in Hartford, 1633-1883*, Hartford, Conn.: Brown & Gross, 1884, pp. 298–299.

Whether any weight is to be laid on those preachings, cryings out, faintings and convulsions which sometimes attend the terrifying language of some preachers and others, as Evidences of or necessary to a genuine conviction of sin, humiliation and preparation for Christ? Agreed in the Negative, as also that there is no weight to be Laid upon those visions or visional discoveries by some of Late pretended to, of Heaven or Hell, or the body or blood of Christ, viz. as represented to the eyes of the body.

Whether the assertion of some Itinerant preachers that the pure gospel and especially the doctrines of Regeneration and Justification by faith are not preached in these churches, their rash censurings of the body of our clergy as Carnal and unconverted men, and notoriously unfit for office is not such a sinful and scandalous violation of the fifth and ninth commandments of the moral Law as ought to be testified against, and such preachers not be admitted to preach in our pulpits and parishes until they have as publickly manifested their repentance as they have given out their false and scandalous assertions? Agreed in the affirmative.

What is to be thought of the religious concern that is this day so general in the Land? Wee trust and believe that the holy Spirit is moving upon the hearts of many, that many have received of late a Saving Change in many of our Towns, and hope and desire that through grace many may yet be savingly wrought upon; but there are sundry things attending this work which are unfruitful and of a dangerous Tendency, and therefore advise both ministers and people in their Respective stations cautiously to guard against everthing of that nature, and wee for ourselves seriously profess our willingness to encourage the good work of God's Spirit agreeable to his Word to the utmost of our power.

11   *Charles Chauncy*
Enthusiasm Described and Caution'd Against (1742)

*Among the ministers of Massachusetts, the Rev. Charles Chauncy
(1705–1787) of the First Church of Boston was a dominant voice for
calm reason and a just, benevolent God. He was not, however, un-
impressed by the revival as it first touched Boston. Jonathan Edwards,
in the most famous sermon of the Awakening (Sinners in the Hands
of an Angry God), told his Enfield, Massachusetts listeners in July
1741 that "there is nothing between you and hell but the air; it is
only the power and mere pleasure of God that holds you up";
Chauncy, at about the same time, was referring to men hanging "as
it were, over the bottomless pit, by the slender thread of life, and the
moment that snaps asunder, you sink into perdition." But appalled by
the extravagances of the Awakening and of awakeners, he soon drew
back and in calm, measured tones—the tones of dispassionate reason—
denounced both.*

I am in the first place, to give you some account of *Enthusiasm.*
And as this is a thing much talk'd of at present, more perhaps
than at any other time that has pass'd over us, it will not be
tho't unseasonable, if I take some pains to let you into a true
understanding of it.

The word, from it's Etymology, carries in it a good meaning,
as signifying *inspiration from* GOD: in which sense, the prophets
under the old testament, and the apostles under the new, might
properly be called *Enthusiasts.* For they were under a divine
influence, spake as moved by the HOLY GHOST, and did such
things as can be accounted for in no way, but by recurring to
an immediate extraordinary power, present with them.

But the word is more commonly used in a bad sense, as in-
tending an *imaginary,* not a *real* inspiration: according to which

SOURCE. Charles Chauncy, *Enthusiasm Described and Caution'd Against,*
Boston: J. Draper for S. Eliot and J. Blanchard, 1742, pp. 3–7, 21–27.

sense, the *Enthusiast* is one, who has a conceit of himself as a person favoured with the extraordinary presence of the *Deity*. He mistakes the workings of his own passions for divine communications, and fancies himself immediately inspired by the SPIRIT of GOD, when all the while, he is under no other influence than that of an over-heated imagination.

The cause of this *enthusiasm* is a bad temperament of the blood and spirits; 'tis properly a disease, a sort of madness: And there are few; perhaps none at all, but are subject to it, tho' none are so much in danger of it as those, in whom *melancholy* is the prevailing ingredient in their constitution. In these it often reigns; and sometimes to so great a degree, that they are really beside themselves, acting as truly by the blind impetus of a wild fancy, as tho' they had neither reason nor understanding.

And various are the ways in which their *enthusiasm* discovers itself.

Sometimes, it may be seen in their countenance. A certain wildness is discernable in their general look and air; especially when their imaginations are mov'd and fired.

Sometimes, it strangely loosens their tongues, and gives them such an energy, as well as fluency and volubility in speaking, as they themselves, by their utmost efforts, can't so much as imitate, when they are not under the enthusiastick influence.

Sometimes, it affects their bodies, throws them into convulsions and distortions, into quakings and tremblings. This was formerly common among the people called *Quakers*. I was myself, when a Lad, an eye witness to such violent agitations and foamings, in a boisterous female speaker, as I could not behold but with surprize and wonder.

Sometimes, it will unaccountably mix itself with their conduct, and give it such a tincture of that which is freakish or furious, as none can have an idea of, but those who have seen the behaviour of a person in a phrenzy.

Sometimes, it appears in their imaginary peculiar intimacy with heaven. They are, in their own opinion, the special favourites of God, have more familiar converse with him than other good men, and receive immediate, extraordinary communications from him. The tho'ts, which suddenly rise up in their

minds, they take for suggestions of the SPIRIT; their very fancies
are divine illuminations; nor are they strongly inclin'd to any
thing, but 'tis an impulse from GOD, a plain revelation of his
will.

And what extravagances, in this temper of mind, are they not
capable of, and under the specious pretext too of paying obedience to the authority of GOD? Many have fancied themselves
acting by immediate warrant from heaven, while they have been
committing the most undoubted wickedness. There is indeed
scarce any thing so wild, either in *speculation* or *practice,* but
they have given into it: They have, in many instances, been
blasphemers of GOD, and open distrubers of the peace of the
world.

But in nothing does the *enthusiasm* of these persons discover
it self more, than in the disregard they express to the Dictates
of *reason.* They are above the force of argument, beyond conviction from a calm and sober address to their understandings.
As for them, they are distinguish'd persons; GOD himself speaks
inwardly and immediately to their souls. . . . And in vain will
you endeavour to convince such persons of any mistakes they are
fallen into. They are certaintly in the right, and know themselves
to be so. They have the SPIRIT opening their understandings
and revealing the truth to them. They believe only as he has
taught them: and to suspect they are in the wrong is to do dishonour to the SPIRIT; 'tis to oppose his dictates, to set up their
own wisdom in opposition to his, and shut their eyes against
that light with which he has shined into their souls. They are
not therefore capable of being argued with; you had as good reason with the wind.

And as the natural consequence of their being thus sure of
every thing, they are not only infinitely stiff and tenacious, but
impatient of contradiction, censorious and uncharitable: they
encourage a good opinion of none but such as are in their way
of thinking and speaking. Those, to be sure, who venture to
debate with them about their errors and mistakes, their weak-
nesses and indiscretions, run the hazard of being stigmatiz'd by
them as poor unconverted wretches, without the SPIRIT, under

the government of carnal reason, enemies to GOD and religion, and in the broad way to hell.

They are likewise positive and dogmatical, vainly fond of their own imaginations, and invincibly set upon propagating them: And in the doing of this, their Powers being awakened, and put as it were, upon the stretch, from the strong impressions they are under, that they are authorized by the immediate command of GOD himself, they sometimes exert themselves with a sort of *extatic* violence: And 'tis this that gives them the advantage, among the less knowing and judicious, of those who are modest, suspicious of themselves, and not too assuming in matters of conscience and salvation. The extraordinary fervour of their minds, accompanied with uncommon bodily motions, and an excessive confidence and assurance gains them great reputation among the populace; who speak of them as *men of* GOD in distinction from all others, and too commonly hearken to, and revere their dictates, as tho' they really were, as they pretend, immediately communicated to them from the DIVINE SPIRIT.

This is the nature of *Enthusiasm,* and this its operation, in a less or greater degree, in all who are under the influence of it. 'Tis a kind of religious Phrenzy, and evidently discovers it self to be so, whenever it rises to any great height.

And much to be pitied are the persons who are seized with it. Our compassion commonly works towards those, who, while under distraction, fondly imagine themselves to be Kings and Emperors: And the like pity is really due to those, who, under the power of *enthusiasm,* fancy themselves to be *prophets; inspired of God,* and *immediately called and commissioned by him to deliver his messages to the world:* And tho' they should run into disorders, and act in a manner that cannot but be condemned, they should notwithstanding be treated with tenderness and lenity; and the rather, because they don't commonly act so much under the influence of a *bad mind,* as a *deluded imagination.* And who more worthy of christian pity than those, who, under the notion of serving GOD and the interest of religion, are filled with zeal, and exert themselves to the utmost, while all the time they are hurting and wounding the very cause they take

so much pains to advance. 'Tis really a pitiable case: And tho'
the honesty of their intentions won't legitimate their bad actions,
yet it very much alleviates their guilt: We should think as fa-
vourably of them as may be, and be dispos'd to judge with
mercy, as we would hope to obtain mercy. . . .

But I shall now draw towards a close, by making some suitable *application* of what has been said, And,

1. Let us beware of charging GOD *foolishly*, from what we
have heard of the *nature*, and *inflence* of *enthusiasm*. This
may appear a dark article in GOD's government of the world; but
it stands upon the same foot with his permission of other evils,
whether *natural* or *moral*. And, if we shou'd not be able to see
perfectly into the reason of this dispensation, we shou'd rather
attribute it to our own ignorance, than reply against GOD. We
may assure ourselves, a wise, and good, and holy GOD, would
not have suffered it thus to be, if there were not some great and
valuable ends to be hereby answered.

Greater advantages may, in the end, accrue to true religion,
by the sufferance of an *enthusiastic* spirit, and the prevalence
of it, at certain times, than we may be capable of discerning at
present.

It may furnish both opportunity and occasion for the trial of
those, who call themselves christians; whether they have just
notions of religion, and courage and faithfulness to stand up for
real truths, against meer *imaginary* ones.—It may serve as a
foil to set off the beauty and glory of true, genuine christianity.—
It may tend to the encouragement of reasonable and solid religion; and, in the run of things, recommend it, in the most
effectual manner, to men's choice and practice.—In a word, It
may put men upon a more thorough examination into the
grounds of the christian religion, and be the means of their being,
more generally, established in its truth, upon the best and most
reasonable evidence. . . .

2. Let none, from what has been offered, entertain prejudices
in their minds against the *operations* of the SPIRIT. There is
such a thing as his influence upon the hearts of men. No consistent sense can be put upon a great part of the *bible*, unless

this be acknowledged for a truth: Nor is it any objection against its being so, that there has been a great deal of *enthusiasm* in the world, many who have mistaken the motions of their own passions for divine operations. This, it must be acknowledged, shou'd make us cautious; putting us upon a careful examination of whatever offers itself, as a communication from the SPIRIT, that we deceive not ourselves: But its no argument, why we shou'd conceive a flighty tho't, either of the SPIRIT, or his influences, really made upon the minds of men. Much less is it a just ground of exception against the SPIRIT's *operations,* that they may be counterfeited; that men may make an appearance, as if they were acted by the SPIRIT, when, all the while, they have no other view in their pretences, but to serve themselves. This has often been the case; and points it out as a matter of necessity, that we take heed to ourselves, if we would not be impos'd upon by a *fair shew,* and *good words:* But at the same time, 'tis no reason why we shou'd think the worse of the blessed SPIRIT, or of those influences that are really *his.* . . .

We must have upon our minds a just tho't of the good SPIRIT, and of his *influences.* This is a matter of necessity. O let us encourage a steady faith in him, as that glorious person, by whom, and by whom alone, we can be prepared in this world, for happiness in the world that is come. And let nothing, no wildness of enthusiasm, ever be able to tempt us to call this in question. And let us so believe in the HOLY GHOST, as to put ourselves under his guidance; and let our dependance be on him for grace to help us in every time of need.

Only let us look to it, that we take no *impressions* for his but such as really are so: And let us not be satisfied, 'till we experience within ourselves the *real effects* of the SPIRIT's operations; such as are common to all that are in CHRIST JESUS; and always have been, and always will be, accompanied with a *holy frame of soul,* and a *conversation becoming the Gospel.*

3. Let not any think *ill* of religion, because of the *ill* representation that is made of it by *enthusiasts.* There may be danger of this; especially, in regard of those who have not upon their minds a serious sense of GOD and the things of another world. They may be ready to judge of religion from the *copy* given

them of it, by those who are too much led by their fancies; and to condemn it, in the gross, as a wild, imaginary, inconsistent thing. But this is to judge too hastily and rashly. Religion ought not to suffer in the opinion of any, because of the imprudencies or extravagancies of those, who call themselves the friends of it. Any thing may be abused: Nor is there any thing, but has actually been abused. And why shou'd any think the worse of religion, because some who make more than ordinary pretences to it, set it forth in an ugly light by their conduct relative to it?

There is such a thing as real religion, let the conduct of men be what it will; and 'tis, in it's nature, a sober, calm, reasonable thing: Nor is it an objection of any weight against the sobriety or reasonableness of it, that there have been *enthusiasts,* who have acted as tho' it was a wild, imaginary business. We should not make our estimate of religion as exhibited in the behaviour of men of a *fanciful* mind; to be sure, we should not take up an ill opinion of it, because in the example they give of it, it don't appear so amiable as we might expect. This is unfair. We shou'd rather judge of it from the conduct of men of a *sound judgment*; whose lives have been such a uniform, beautiful transcript of that which is just and good, that we can't but think well of religion, as display'd in their example. . . .

4. Let us esteem those as *friends* to religion, and not *enemies,* who warn us of the danger of *enthusiasm,* and wou'd put us upon our guard, that we be not led aside by it. As the times are, they run the hazard of being call'd *enemies* to the *holy* SPIRIT, and may expect to be ill-spoken of by many, and loaded with names of reproach: But they are notwithstanding the best friends to religion; and it may be, it will more and more appear, that they have all along been so. They have been stigmatised as OPPOSERS of the WORK OF GOD; but 'tis a great mercy of GOD, there have been such OPPOSERS: This land had, in all probability, been over-run with confusion and distraction, if they had acted under the influence of the same *heat* and *zeal,* which some others have been famous for.

'Tis really best, people shou'd know there is such a thing as *enthusiasm,* and that it has been, in all ages, one of the most dangerous enemies to the church of GOD, and has done a world of mischief: And 'tis a kindness to them to be warn'd against it, and directed to the proper methods to be preserved from it. 'Tis indeed, one of the best ways of doing service to *real* religion, to distinguish it from that which is *imaginary:* Nor shou'd ministers be discouraged from endeavouring this, tho' they shou'd be ill-tho't, or evil-spoken of. They shou'd beware of being too much under the influence of that *fear of man, which bringeth a snare;* which is evidently the case, where they are either silent, or dare not speak out faithfully and plainly, lest they shou'd be called PHARISEES or HYPOCRITES, and charged with LEADING SOULS TO THE DEVIL. 'Tis a *small matter* to be thus *judged* and *reviled;* and we shou'd be above being affrighted from duty by this, which is nothing more than the *breath* of poor, ignorant, frail man.

There is, I doubt not, a great deal of *real, substantial* religion in the land. The SPIRIT of GOD has wro't effectually on the hearts of many, from one time to another: And I make no question he has done so of late, in more numerous instances, it may be, than usual. But this, notwithstanding, there is, without dispute, a *spirit of enthusiasm,* appearing in one place and another. There are those, who make great pretences to the SPIRIT, who are carried away with their imaginations: And some, it may be, take themselves to be *immediately and wonderfully conducted by him;* while they are led only by their own fancies.

Thus it has been in other parts of the world. *Enthusiasm,* in all the *wildness,* and *fury,* and *extravagance* of it, has been among them, and sometimes had a most dreadfully extensive spread. *Ten thousand* wild *enthusiasts* have appear'd in arms, at the same time; and this too, in defence of *gross opinions,* as well as *enormous actions.* The first discovery therefore of such a spirit, unless due care is taken to give check to its growth and progress, is much to be feared; for there is no knowing, how high it may rise, nor what it may end in.—

The good LORD give us all wisdom; and courage, and conduct, in such a Day as this! And may both *ministers* and *people* behave after such a manner, as that religion may not suffer; but in the end, gain advantage, and be still more universally established.

And, may that grace of GOD, which has appeared to all men, bringing salvation, teach us effectually, to deny ungodliness and worldly lusts, and to live soberly, and righteously, and godlily in the world: so may we look with comfort for the appearing of our SAVIOUR JESUS CHRIST: And when he shall appear in the glory of his FATHER, and with his holy angels, we also shall appear with him, and go away into everlasting life: Which GOD, of his infinite mercy grant may be the portion of us all; for the sake of CHRIST JESUS.

12 The Canterbury, Connecticut Church and Mr. Adams (1743)

Within the churches themselves the dispute raged as (among Presbyterians) New Side and Old Side and (in New England) New Lights and Old Lights battled each other. Churches and denominations divided and individual congregations accepted or rejected their ministers almost at will. The complicated quarrels of Canterbury, Connecticut are not in themselves important. But the account of the interrogation of a prospective minister for the church by a committee of the congregation displays the spirit of the moment and some of the issues. In this particular case the congregation was dominated by New Lights (the awakened) and the prospective minister, one Mr. Adams, was Old Light. Mr. Adams was not hired.

To the Church of Christ now met by adjournment:—

Dearly Beloved: According to your order, we, the subscribers, waited upon Mr. Adams, informed him that the church was dissatisfied, and gave him a copy of the church's vote concerning his sermons, I. Cor. x: 31, and in answer to what the church

SOURCE. Report of a committee of the Canterbury Church of Christ, September 7, 1743, in Ellen D. Larned, *History of Windham County, Connecticut, I, 1600–1760*, Worcester, Mass.: published by the author, 1874, pp. 405–406.

saith of the general run of said sermons (in that they imply
that man hath a power to glorify God, not implying that the
new birth is necessary) he saith, "That he was preaching to
Christians, and they had passed through the new birth, and
therefore it was not needful to show the necessity of it." We
asked him, "Whether he thought that all who heard him were
such?"

ADAMS: "No! but all that I directed my discourse to were."

COMMITTEE: "It did not appear so by the terms used in addressing them."

A: "In opening the text, I did show that the Apostle writ to the
Christians at Corinth, and that showed that I was preaching to
Christians. Is not that true?"

C: "It is true the *Apostle* did as you say, but in your doctrine,
the foundation of your discourse, you address them under the
general denomination of men, which is not peculiar to Christians,
but when it is used by way of distinction it denotes men in
their natural estate."

A: "Women heard me, too, and you may say I did not preach
to *them* because I did not call them women."

C: "Preaching up duty and works as terms of life is dangerous."

A: "I did not say they were terms of life but what Christians
ought to do because they were redeemed, which I laid down as
an obligation to obedience, and also showed that I was showing
Christians their duty, and ought they not to do those duties that
I laid down?"

C: "Many of them were duties that ought to be done, and the
doing of them to be pressed upon Christians, but you did not
show that faith in Jesus Christ and the love of God in the soul
were absolutely necessary in order to glorify God in doing them."

A: "I did mention faith and love, with several other things,
as necessary."

C: "But inasmuch as you put them with several other things,
and then said that all or some of them were necessary, you so
left it in your sermon that people might take the other and leave
out faith and love, as not being so absolutely necessary."

A: "I could not help that, and nobody would take my sermons as the church hath represented, except they were prejudiced against me."

c: "Some that like your preaching *have* taken it so, and say they are of opinion that if a man doth what he can he shall be accepted."

A: "You need not fear it hurting *you, knowing you are converted* as you say."

c: "Our hearts are so apt to deceive us on that point, we earnestly desire to have the Word divided aright after we have been enlightened and sanctified in part, but we look upon it most dangerous for those poor souls that are dead in sins, for they know of no other way but to do and live. . . . One of us was discoursing with a man in this town concerning that point, and the man said, 'That God doth not require anything of any man but what he hath given power to do.' "

A: "It *is* true that God hath given him power to do all that he requires of him."

c: "Has God given every man power to believe?"

A: "Was any man ever lost who did what he could to save himself, or towards his own salvation?"

When we had heard what he, as above-written, saith to the general expression the church had taken, we then discoursed of the particulars that were in themselves contrary to sound doctrine, viz., that it is not necessary in every particular to [have perfect sinless obedience for] the Glory of God, and he, to rectifie that point asked, "Whether perfect sinless obedience was required under the Gospel?"

c: "Nothing but a perfect righteousness would be accepted."

A: "We are not under the Law, but under Grace."

c: "Shall we continue in sin because we are not under the Law?"

A: "No. But would you have me preach that man must have a perfect sinless obedience?"

c: "They must aim at and endeavor after it, but it is in their aims that you have left such room, and that makes it the more dangerous, and in your saying that it matters not much whether a man knows precisely whether the reward of happiness or the glory of God be the chief motive to put him upon doing, &c., we look upon it to be the more dangerous, because we are of opinion that that is the most necessary and most difficult point to know in self-examination."

A: "What goes before and follows after in my sermon guards against this danger."

C: "You have not said anything in your sermons that implied that there were any that were in danger of perishing in the state they were in."

A: "I did, in showing how they should come to God, imply that as plainly as if I had said it in plain words."

C: "But you did not tell them they had no legs nor power to come, and they were dead."

A: "Christians have legs, and such I was preaching to."

We informed him that the church would meet on this day, and we desired him to be present at this meeting. He said he was going out of town. We asked him what answer we should give the church on the premises. He said, he cared not what, and left us.

SOLOMON PAINE.

THOMAS BRADFORD.

BENAJAH DOUGLAS.

13   *James Davenport*
Confession and Retractions (1744)

The Rev. James Davenport (1716–1757) was among the most enthusiastic of the awakeners, and much of the criticism of such men as Chauncy was prompted by his activities. Even Davenport's fellow awakeners were critical of his antics, holding him largely responsible for both the growing attack on enthusiasm and an appreciable slackening of ardor that was to be noted in New England and the middle

SOURCE. *The Reverend Mr. James Davenport's Confession & Retractions,* Boston: S. Kneeland and T. Green, 1744, pp. 3–8.

colonies by mid–1743. Davenport had begun his ministry in Southhold, Long Island in 1738, been swept into revivalism by Whitefield himself, traveled extensively through Connecticut, Massachusetts, New York and New Jersey, and climaxed his career in March 1743 by compelling a band of the converted in New London, Connecticut, to burn their fine clothes and ornaments, and even their books—the smoke of the bonfire reminding Davenport of the eternal torment that certain of his enemies must surely suffer in hell. Twice arrested and twice judged insane (by the civil authorities of Connecticut and Massachusetts respectively), he was finally brought to recant his excesses by the pressure of both friends and foes. Davenport's recanting symbolically ends the awakening per se, the period of near-chaotic itinerancy, and opens a period of retrenchment and organization as the awakened began to formalize their new churches and new denominations.

Altho' I don't question at all, but there is great Reason to bless God for a *glorious and wonderful Work of his Power and Grace* in the *Edification* of his Children, and the *Conviction* and *Conversion* of Numbers in *New-England,* in the *neighbouring Governments & several other Parts,* within a few Years past; and believe that the Lord hath favoured me, tho' most unworthy, with several others of his Servants, in granting special Assistance and Success; the Glory of all which be given to Jᴇʜᴏᴠᴀʜ, to whom alone it belongs:

Yet after frequent Meditation and Desires that I might be enabled to apprehend Things justly, and, I hope I may say, mature Consideration; I am now fully convinced and perswaded that *several Appendages* to *this glorious Work* are no essential Parts thereof, but of a *different* and *contrary* Nature and Tendency; *which Appendages* I have been in the Time of the Work very industrious in and instrumental of promoting, by a misguided Zeal: being further much influenced in the Affair by the *false Spirit;* which, unobserved by me, did (as I have been brought to see since) prompt me to *unjust Apprehensions* and *Misconduct in several Articles;* which have been great Blemishes to the Work of God, very grievous to some of God's Children, no less in sharing and corrupting to others of them, a sad Means of many Persons questioning the Work of God, concluding and appearing against it, and of the hardening of Multitudes in their Sins, and an awful Occasion of the Enemies blaspheming the right Ways of the Lord; and withal very offensive to that God, before whom I would lie in the Dust, prostrate in deep Humility and Repentance on this Account, imploring Pardon for the Mediator's Sake, and thankfully accepting the Tokens thereof.

The *Articles,* which I especially refer to, and would in the most public Manner *retract,* and *warn others against,* are these which follow *viz.*

I. The Method I us'd for a considerable Time, with Respect to some, yea many *Ministers* in several Parts, in openly *exposing such as I fear'd or thought unconverted, in publick Prayer or otherwise:* herein making my private Judgment, (in which also I much suspect I was mistaken in several Instances, and I believe also that my Judgment concerning several, was formed rashly and upon very slender Grounds.) I say, making my private Judgment, the Ground of publick Actions or Conduct; offending, as I apprehend (altho' in the Time of it ignorantly) against the *ninth Commandment,* and such other Passages of Scripture, as are similar; yea, I may say, offending against the Laws both of Justice and Charity: Which Laws were further broken

II. By my *advising and urging to such Separations* from *those Ministers,* whom I treated as above, as I believe may be justly called rash, unwarrantable, and of sad and awful Tendency and Consequence. And here I would ask the Forgiveness of those Ministers, whom I have injured in both these Articles.

III. I confess I have been much led astray by *following Impulses* or Impressions as a Rule of Conduct, whether they came with or without a Text of Scripture; and my neglecting also duly to observe the Analogy of Scripture: I am perswaded this was a great Means of corrupting my Experiences and carrying me off from the Word of God, and a great Handle, which the *false Spirit* has made use of with Respect to a Number, and me especially.

IV. I believe further that I have done much Hurt to Religion by *encouraging private Persons to a ministerial and authoritative Kind or Method of exhorting;* which is particularly observable in many such being much puft up and *falling into the Snare of the Devil,* whilst many others are thus directly prejudic'd against the Work.

V. I have Reason to be deeply humbled that I have not been duly careful to endeavour to remove or prevent Prejudice, (where I now believe I might then have done it consistently with Duty) which appear'd remarkable in the Method I practis'd, of *singing with others in the Streets* in Societies frequently.

I would also penitently confess and bewail my *great Stiffness* in retaining these *aforesaid Errors* a great while, and unwillingness to examine into them with any Jealousy of their being Errors, notwithstanding the friendly Counsels and Cautions of real Friends, especially in the Ministry.

Here may properly be added a Paragraph or two, taken out of a *Letter from me* to Mr. *Barber* at *Georgia;* a *true Copy* of which I gave Consent should be publish'd lately at *Philadelphia:* "——I would add to what Brother *T*——— hath written on the awful Affair of Books and Cloaths at *New-London,* which affords Grounds of deep and lasting Humiliation; I was to my Shame be it spoken, the Ringleader in *that horrid Action; I* was, my dear Brother, under the powerful Influence of the *false Spirit* almost one whole Day together, and Part of several Days. The Lord shewed me afterwards that the Spirit I was then acted by was in it's Operations void of true inward Peace, laying the greatest Stress on Externals, neglecting the Heart, full of Impatience, Pride and Arrogance; altho' I thought in the Time of it, that 'twas the Spirit of God in an high Degree; awful indeed! my Body especially my Leg much disorder'd at the same Time, which Satan and my evil Heart might make some handle of.——"

And now may the holy wise and good God, be pleas'd to guard and secure me against *such Errors* for the future, and stop the Progress of those, whether Ministers or People, who have been corrupted by my Words or Example in any of the above-mention'd Particulars; and if it be his holy Will, bless *this publick Recantation* to this Purpose. And Oh! may he grant withal, that such as by Reason of the aforesaid *Errors and Mis-*

conduct have entertained unhappy Prejudices against Christianity in general, or the late glorious Work of God in particular, may by this Account learn to distinguish the *Appendage* from the *Substance* or *Essence,* that which is *vile* and *odious* from that which is *precious, glorious* and *divine,* and thus be intirely and happily freed from all those Prejudices refer'd to, and this in infinite Mercy through Jesus Christ: and to these Requests may all God's Children, whether Ministers or others say, *Amen.*

    July 28. 1744.

James Davenport.

THE DIVINE MISSION

14   *Samuel Finley*
Christ Triumphing (1741)

*The Great Awakening was not an event out of context. It had
origins inherent in the setting and it had an aftermath. In one sense
the aftermath can be seen in the formalization of new religious institutions and in the continuing struggle between these new institutions
and the old. In another sense, the aftermath lay in the resuscitation
of basic Calvinism in America and in the tradition of revivalism that
entered American religious life, for revivals were to recur time and
time again. But in still a third sense it lay in the rationalizations of
religious enthusiasm that were prompted by the attacks upon the
awakeners, rationalizations that evoked millenarianism—"Christ's kingdom is come!"—and a peculiar American nationalism—"It is come
here!" The defense written by Samuel Finley (1715–1766) is note-
worthy in this respect. Born in Ireland, he came to the colonies in
1734, studied with the Tennents, and became an itinerant in 1740.
Eventually he became president of the College of New Jersey at
Princeton—a post held also by Jonathan Edwards and Samuel Davies.*

All that remains now of the Doctrinal Part, is . . . To prove,
That the Kingdom of God is come unto us at this Day.

SOURCE. Samuel Finley, *Christ Triumphing and Satan Raging. A Sermon
on Matth. xii. 28. Wherein is Proven, that the Kingdom of God Is Come
Unto Us at This Day*, Philadelphia: B. Franklin, 1741, pp. 23–32.

Oh the joyful Sound! *Unto us,* upon whom the Ends of the World are come! Surely all that hear me will rejoice, if I can make it appear.

That there has been a great religious Commotion in the World in our present Day, is so evident, that it cannot be deny'd: But there has been a Murmuring among the People; some saying, That God is with us of a Truth; that the Day spring from on high has visited us; and the Day-star has risen in many Hearts: Others saying, Nay, it is all Deceit, or Delusion, or the Work of the Devil. But that Christ is come to his Church, will appear, I presume, in the Judgment of any considering Person, If I can make these Things appear.

1. That the Church was in the same Circumstances as when he us'd to visit it.

2. If the Manner of his Coming be in Substance the same.

3. If the Treatment he meets with, be the same.

4. If the Consequences and Effects be the same.

5. If the Attempts and Objections made against him, be the same. And, in a Word,

If the Devil be cast out by Means of true Gospel-Doctrine.

And 1. As to the Circumstances of the Church; He always came when it needed a Reformation, even in the Judgment of graceless Professors; when Religion dwindled into an empty Form, and Professors had lost the Life and Power of Godliness; in a Word, when there was Midnight-Darkness, and little Faith to be found on the Earth. Thus it was when he came in the Flesh; when he sent St. *Athanasius, Luther* and *Calvin,* and at the Reformation of Scotland. We find the graceless *Jews* prayed for the Day of the Lord, in *Amos* 5. 18. And hence were our Pulpits filled with seemingly devout Prayers for a Revival of Religion, and Confessions of its decayed State. And what had we lately but a dry Formality? Did not all in general seem to be at Ease in *Zion,* and in much Peace about the State of their Souls? How few are asking the Watch-men, *What of the*

Night? The Lives of Professors careless, unholy, unguarded; Ordinances attended, Duties performed, Sermons preached, without Life or Power, and as little Success. Was not worldly Discourse our mutual Entertainment at our solemn Assemblies on Holy-days? Thus in Darkness and Security were we: And *like People, like Priest.*

2. As to the Manner of his Coming; It never was in such a Manner as carnal Persons imagined; but still unexpected and out of the common Way. And this is a necessary Consequent of the State of the Church: For since he comes in a dark Time, we may easily conclude, that the Manner thereof is unobserv'd at first. He must needs come unawares, when a carnal World have forgotten, and do neglect him; and do not know him, or the powerful Operations of his Spirit untill they feel them. For tho' they may pray for the Day of the Lord; yet they know it not when it comes, and so do not know what they ask. *Amos* 5. 18. Now, by this Means he comes always quite cross to the Inclinations of the Clergy, who are generally sunk in Carnality as well as the People. And as a Consequence of this, the Ministers by whom He works, have always at first been few: And thus the Work appears the more eminently to be his own, the less probable that the Instruments appear. Thus it was when he came in the Flesh, He came indeed out of *Bethlehem.* but in a mean Condition; and afterwords unperceivably changing his Place, was mistaken. When he enter'd on his publick Ministry, it was not according to the Traditions of the Fathers; for we find they were surprized, in *Luke* iv. when he began to expound the Scriptures, being neither a Scribe nor Pharisee. And the People not being used with such close and particular Applications, could not bear his new Methods. Passing by the established, but proud, bigotted, gainsaying Clergy, he chuses Twelve unlearned, unpolished Men, most of them Fishers; and gave them a Commission to preach the Gospel, without consulting the *Sanhedrim* about such *unprecedented* Proceedings. Thus was his coming dark, and cross to them.—Now, in our Days the parallel is plain, for supposing the present Commotion to be the Work of God: Every one knows how cross it is to the Inclinations of the Clergy. Surely, our Opposers will confess, they neither did,

nor do expect Religion to be reviv'd in such a Manner; while they are so many Things, in their Opinion, wrong. Surely, it is a dark Day to them, and no Light in it; many of them know not what to make of it, by their own Confession. We all know how few it's Propagators are; and they say, that most of us are unlearned: But do they not, by the by, bewray themselves herein? For if unlearned, they must have the less Rhetorick & Oratory; and consequently the less able to bring such Things to pass. If it were the Work of Man, a superior Power of Man would overthrow it.—In a Word, the parallel holds in every Thing, only our manner of Licensing is not *unprecedented*.

3. The Treatment he met with; as a native Consequence of his coming in so dark and mean a Condition, and cross to the Minds of the Clergy; he was rejected by them, and by many of the Noble and Mighty after the Flesh; who imbitter'd against him as many People as they could influence. And as a Consequence of his being disown'd by these, he was chiefly followed by what we call the *Mob,* the *Rabble,* the *common* and *meaner* Sort. And being disown'd by the self-righteous Moralists, was follow'd by the openly profane, the *Publicans,* and *Harlots;* for he is still set for the *Rise & Fall of many in* Israel; and many who tho't themselves *first,* and were esteemed so by others in the Dark, did show themselves to be *last.* Thus it was when he came in the Flesh; rejected by the Clergy so generally, and by the Noble and Wise, that it was said, *Have any of the Rulers or Pharisees believed on him?* No: *But this People who know not the Law, are accursed.*—Just so is he treated by the same Ranks of Persons at this Day. May I not ask, Have any of the Rulers, have any of the Ministers embraced the present Work? Do they not rather prepossess & imbitter the carnal People against it? And many who seemed *first* in Religion, are they not become the very *last,* and the *last, first?* For our Opposers confess of their own Accord, That *it is only the ignorant Rabble that embrace it; many of which never minded any Religion, & so do not know the Law.* Sure they who know the Law, might know that it is a good Proof of a Day of God's Power when *the Poor have the Gospel preach'd to them,* and do receive it. Mat. xi. 5. Might they not know that our Lord used this Argument? And

also that *God chuses foolish Things to confound the Wise?* But they must confess, that tho' there be not *many,* yet, Glory to God! there are *some* of the *Wise,* and *Mighty,* and *Noble,* on our Side.

4. The Effects & Consequences of his Coming; as a Consequence of the strong Opposition of the Clergy, & others of their Adherents, against him. Contrary to their own Intention, their Speaking of him was a Means of setting the People on the Search; and Numbers flock'd after him, to hear these new *Doctrines* and *new Methods;* and were then caught in the Gospel-net: *As many as were ordained to eternal Life, believed.* Thus in Joh. vii. 11, & *seq.* the Pharisees speaking against him, put him in the People's Minds, who began to talk of him. His Audiences were often deeply affected; and frequently divided between him and the Clergy: And hence we so often read, that *there was a Division among the People.* He never came to send Peace on the Earth, but a *Sword, & Division.* Luke xii. 51-58.—Just so it has been in our Day. Many can say by Experience, that their Attention and Curiosity was raised by Means of the Contradictions of their Ministers. And hence we have seen unusual Numbers going to hear the Word like thirsty Flocks: And heard a great Mourning, like the Mourning of *Hadadrimmon* in the Valley of *Megiddon.* Also there has been a Division among the Peoples; some praising God for what their Eyes have seen, & their Ears heard, & their Souls felt; others going away mocking, contradicting, blaspheming.

Another Effect was, the Breaking down of Bigotry; partly as a native consequence of the Attention of all Parties being raised to come and hear; and partly by the Example and Directions of Christ, and his Followers. Thus he freely conversed, eat and drank, with different opposite Parties, *Jews & Samaritans, Publicans* and *Pharisees;* and justified his so doing from the Need there was of it, that all might come freely and reap Benefit. And the Apostle, in *Phil.* iii. 15, 16. advises real Christians who hold the Foundation, to walk together in such Things as they are agreed in; for in Things wherein they are disagreed, they cannot.—And just so our Opposers confess it to be now, while they accuse us for holding Communion with different Societies, and would insinuate, that we do so from some politick Design: Indeed there is this Policy in it, to gain some by any Means, and make a Party for Jesus Christ.

5. The Attempts; as a Consequence of the People's following Christ or his Ambassadors, and disregarding the Clergy, the latter always attempted to overthrow the new Scheme; Were (1) unwearied in forming mischievious Devices against him; would tell the People, they had an Imposture, and were deluded, and deceiv'd; follow'd him for no other End but to find something to cavil at; wrested both his Words and Actions to find Matter of Accusation. (2) They were unsatisfied; for after they had been busy all along, they say, *What do we?* q.d. [*quasi dicat,* as if he should say] We have been too slack & cowardly; come, let us bestir ourselves, & not suffer all to be overturn'd; we have prevail'd nothing as yet. (3) Their Attempts were still unsuccessful, and always tended to promote the Cause they were set to baffle: Tho' they are still busy, yet are conscious they prevail nothing. Thus when the Scribes & Pharisees sought Christ at the Feast, *John* vii. 11. they put him in the People's Minds, who straight began to talk of him, some good, some evil: When the Pharisees perceived this, they forbid them to speak of him either good or ill; for so much is imply'd in these Words, *Howbeit no Man spoke openly of him for Fear of the Jews.* They hoped that the Thoughts of Christ would wear out of the People's Minds thro' Time.—Just thus do the Opposers now to a tittle. It can be made appear, how Companies of Ministers & People, have met together in a private Manner, to consult how they might suppress the *new Scheme,* and what they could say against it: And indeed, their Cavils, & the Spirit with which they are urged, do plainly show, that they rather desire Matter of Accusation, than that they really have it. How do they twist and wrest both the Words and Actions, and magnify the Blemishes, of those who stand up for the Work of God? If they can find an unguarded Expression, they draw what horrid Consequences from it they can, & then affirm that this is the Man's Principles. They want some plausible Pretence to blind the People. And they are yet saying, *What do we?*—And I could show, were it necessary, how every Instance of Opposition against the present

Work, have all been turn'd to its Advantage. Oh that they would consider whom they fight against! for God is with us of a Truth. And now some of them beg for Peace, and would have us be silent about these controverted Things, that they may wear out of Mind. Their asking Peace & Quietness has an Aspect pleasing to the Flesh, and looks plausible: But God forbid that we should cease to proclaim his wondrous Deeds, to humour the Enemies of his Work! No; let us tell them abroad more loudly, tho' it gall the Consciences, & torment the Minds of all the Opposers on Earth, *Rev.* xi. 10. Thus far we are on a straight Parallel, by the Confession of our Opposers.

6. The Objections made against Him, are the same as usual.

For, (1) The Pharisees objected Disorder to our Lord, & his Apostles. How often are they accused of not walking according to the Traditions of the Elders? And our Opposers say, This cannot be the Work of God, because not according to their Order: But they proved not that God is oblig'd to work by their Rules.

(2) When our Lord & his Apostles pleaded for free Grace, they were called Enemies to *Moses* and the Law; and he was often call'd a Blasphemer. So the present Opposers of God's Work, accuse some of us of speaking against the Law, & call us *Antinomians;* and tug & strive, by wresting both the Words and Intentions of some of our Brethren, to prove them Blasphemy. *He hath spoken Blasphemy, why hear ye him?*

(3) It was objected to our Lord and his Apostles, that they held Communion with Persons of different Societies. Hence they stumbled, because he kept Company with *Publicans,* and *Samaritans,* and *Sinners.* And tho't, had he been so much as a common Prophet, he would have known better what Company to keep; and hence concluded he could not possibly be the Christ.—So our Opposers say, that we bring the Church into Confusion by a mixt Communion of different Perswasions; who yet hold the Foundation. And further they ask, Why these who were of no religious Society, are fond of this *new Scheme? Why eateth your Master with Publicanes and Sinners?* He that pretends to be so good a Man, why does he keep such bad Com-

pany? They seem now to think it unjust, that Persons who never did so much in Religion as they should enter into the Kingdom of Heaven before them.

(4) It is objected to us, that this Commotion rends the Church; divides Congregations and Families; sets People at Variance; makes them harsh and censorious. So we hear *Tertullus,* Acts xxiv. 5. accuse *Paul* as a *pestilent Fellow, a Mover of Sedition, a Profaner of the Temple.* The Pharisees, *John* ix. 44. ask in a sour Manner, *Are we blind also?* Dost thou judge us to be blind too so rashly? And *Elijah,* because a Son of Thunder, tho' he was the most peaceable, yet he must needs be call'd a *Troubler of Israel,* in I Kin. xviii. 17. And in a Word, both they and we are Turners of the World upside down, Subverters of Peace and Church-Government, and the like. Luke xii. 51. 57. *Suppose ye, says Christ, that I am come to send Peace on the Earth? I came not to send Peace, but a Sword; to divide a Family against it self.—Why cannot* our present Opposers *discern the Signs of* THESE TIMES?

(5) The present Opposers say, they do not quarrel with these Disorders. So, in *John* x. 33. the *Jews* say, *For a good Work we stone thee not:* No: far be it from us, do not so mistake us, we would be ready to encourage every Thing that has the Appearance of Piety; 'tis not for thy good Works, *but for Blasphemy.* But his good Works, instead of procuring their Favour, did raise their Envy: yet they could willingly have embrued their Hands in his Blood, for no other Crime but his good Works; because he so far out-shined them. But on account of the People, they must first find some plausible Pretence against him. They took no Notice, or laid no Stress on his Miracles; were never satisfied with all the Evidences he gave them; their common Question was, *What Sign showest thou?* Though they seemed resolved not to be satisfied with any Sign. They still found Exceptions against all his Works; and when they could not deny the Matter of Fact, they ascribe it to the Devil sometimes. How often do they ask the Man born blind, how he received his Sight? and would willingly have deny'd that he was blind: How earnest were they to find some Flaw or other? And when they could find none, they put a religious Face upon

their Envy; exhort the Man to give God the Glory, but not to mind Jesus; for they were sure he was a Sinner.—Just so it is now a days to a Tittle. Our Opposers have no End of asking for Evidences; without taking Notice of the Power of God, that has appear'd in the Assemblies, or on the Lives of Men: They still muster up Objections, and harp only on what they call Disorder. They gather a great many of their Exceptions together, and then ask, if these Irregularities be the Work of God. Without observing the deep Concern that Souls seem to be under, they only ask about the *Fits* and *Convulsions* that their Sorrow throw them into; and which they would be ready to allow for, in worldly Respects, as the sudden News of the Death of Friends, or the like. And if some unexceptionable Evidence of the Power of God, be alledged against them; they strive to evade its Force some Way or other, by saying, That possibly God may bring Good out of Evil; but yet do they speak against the Whole, as a Devilish Work. They seem glad to get any objection against it; not willing that it should be the Work of God. They fix their Eyes only on the Failures & Blemishes of those who defend it, and magnify Mole-hills into Mountains: And if they can get nothing that has the Appearance of a Fault, they are industrious to forge, and spread slanderous Reports, and false Insinuations; and seem as fond of them, as if they had got a Victory. In a Word; they appear as if their greatest Desire was, to blind their own Eyes, & stop their own Ears, that hearing they might not understand, and seeing they might not perceive, lest they should be *Converts* too, as they call us by the Way of Ridicule.

Thus the Parallel runs clear and undeniable. The same Attempts and Objections, from the same Ranks of Persons, do prove the same Dispositions to be in graceless Persons, now, as formerly; the same Blindness & Enmity. And why should it be tho't strange that Christ's pretended Ambassadors are his bitterest Enemies, seeing it has been always so? The Lord always reformed his Church contrary to their Desires. There is the same kind of Opposition, & Opposers too, in *Scotland* & *England,* at present as here in *America.* And had I Time, I could show,

that all Things in every Period of the Church, answer & agree
with this, as Face answers to Face in a Glass. But the Coming
of Christ in the Flesh, will be found to be analogous to his
Coming at other Times; & the Parellel from that is most level
to the Capacity of every one; and trac'd with less Difficulty, &
more Certainty by common People: And therefore I have chiefly
compared that Period, and our present Day.

15 *Jonathan Edwards*
Some Thoughts Concerning the Present Revival
of Religion (1742)

*Writing also in the heat of dispute, Jonathan Edwards defended the
Awakening. Edwards was to write a tremendous amount in the years
after the Awakening until his death in 1758, much of it in elaborate
defense of the basic principles that underlay the revivalists' concern
for conversion. But the 378–page polemic—an extension of an earlier
sermon—that he published in Boston late in 1742 has been called by
one leading scholar (Alan Heimert in* The Great Awakening, *Indianapolis and New York: Bobbs-Merrill Company, 1967) "the major document of the Awakening" and "one of Edwards' most significant utterances." Heimert states, "Here he drew together for the first time in a
single treatise evangelical doctrine, psychological insight, and historical
vision. At the center of all was Edwards' dramatic and unforgettable
prophecy of the New World's spiritual destiny."*

All will allow that true virtue or holiness has its seat chiefly
in the heart, rather than in the head: it therefore follows, from
what has been said already, that it consists chiefly in holy af-

SOURCE. Jonathan Edwards, *Some Thoughts Concerning the Present Revival of Religion in New England* (Boston: S. Kneeland and T. Green,
1742), in *The Works of President Edwards*, New York: Leavitt, Trow & Co.,
1844, III, pp. 280–282, 285, 313–316.

fections. The things of religion take place in men's hearts, no further than they are *affected* with them. The informing of the understanding is all vain, any farther than it *affects* the heart; or which is the same thing, has influence on the *affections*.

Those gentlemen that make light of these raised affections in religion, will doubtless allow that true religion and holiness, as it has its seat in the heart, is capable of very high degrees, and high exercises in the soul. As for instance; they will doubtless allow that the holiness of the heart or will, is capable of being raised to a hundred times as great a degree of strength as it is in the most eminent saint on earth, or to be exerted in a hundred times so strong and vigorous exercises of the heart; and yet be true religion or holiness still, but only in a high degree. Now therefore I would ask them, by what name they will call these high and vigorous exercises of the will or heart? Are they not high affections? What can they consist in, but in high acts of love; strong and vigorous exercises of benevolence and complacence; high, exalting and admiring thoughts of God and his perfections; strong desires after God? &c. And now what are we come to but high and raised affections? Yea, those very same high and raised affections that before they objected against, or made light of, as worthy of little regard?

I suppose furthermore that all will allow that there is nothing but solid religion in heaven: but that there, religion and holiness of heart is raised to an exceeding great height, to strong, high, exalted exercises of heart. Now, what other kinds of such exceeding strong and high exercises of the heart, or of holiness, as it has its seat in their hearts, can we devise for them, but only holy affections, high degrees of actings of love to God, rejoicing in God, admiring of God? &c. Therefore these things in the saints and angels in heaven, are not to be despised and cashiered by the name of great heats and transports of the passions.

And it will doubtless be yet further allowed, that the more eminent the saints are on earth, and the stronger their grace is, and the higher its exercises are, the more they are like the saints in heaven; i.e., (by what has been just now observed) the more they have of high or raised affections in religion.

Though there are false affections in religion, and affections that in some respects are raised high, that are flashy, yet undoubtedly there are also true, holy and solid affections; and the higher these are raised, the better: and if they are raised to an exceeding great height, they are not to be thought meanly of or suspected, merely because of their great degree, but, on the contrary, to be esteemed and rejoiced in. Charity or divine love, is in Scripture represented as the sum of all the religion of the heart; but this is nothing but a holy *affection:* and therefore in proportion as this is firmly fixed in the soul, and raised to a great height, the more eminent a person is in holiness. Divine love or charity is represented as the sum of all the religion of heaven, and that wherein mainly the religion of the church in its more perfect state on earth shall consist, when knowledge and tongues, and phrophesyings shall cease; and therefore the higher this holy affection is raised in the church of God, or in a gracious soul, the more excellent and perfect is the state of the church, or a particular soul.

If we take the Scriptures for our rule then, the greater and higher are the exercises of love to God, delight and complacence in God, desires and longings after God, delight in the children of God, love to mankind, brokenness of heart, abhorrence of sin, and self-abhorrence for sin; and the peace of God, which passeth all understanding, and joy in the Holy Ghost, joy unspeakable and full of glory; admiring thoughts of God, exulting and glorifying in God; so much the higher is Christ's religion, or that virtue which he and his apostles taught, raised in the soul.

It is a stumbling to some that religious affections should seem to be so powerful, or that they should be so violent (as they express it) in some persons: they are therefore ready to doubt whether it can be the Spirit of God, or whether this vehemence be not rather a sign of the operation of an evil spirit. But why should such a doubt arise from no other ground than this? What is represented in Scripture, as more powerful in its effects, than the Spirit of God? . . .

2. Many are guilty of not taking the holy Scriptures as a sufficient and whole rule, whereby to judge of this work, whether

it be the work of God, in that they judge by those things which the Scripture does not give as any signs or marks whereby to judge one way or the other, and therefore do in no wise belong to the Scripture rule of judging, viz., the effects that religious exercises and affections of mind have upon the body. Scripture rules respect the state of the mind, and persons' moral conduct, and voluntary behavior, and not the physical state of the body. The design of the Scripture is to teach us divinity, and not physic and anatomy. Ministers are made the watchmen of men's souls, and not of their bodies; and therefore the great rule which God has committed into their hands, is to make them divines, and not physicians. Christ knew what instructions and rules his church would stand in need of better than we do; and if he had seen it needful in order to the church's safety, he doubtless would have given ministers rules to judge of bodily effects, and would have told them how the pulse should beat under such and such religious exercises of mind; when men should look pale, and when they should shed tears; when they should tremble, and whether or no they should ever be faint or cry out; or whether the body should ever be put into convulsions: he probably would have put some book into their hands, that should have tended to make them excellent anatomists and physicians: but he has not done it, because he did not see it to be needful. He judged, that if ministers thoroughly did their duty as watchmen and over-seers of the state and frame of men's souls, and of their voluntary conduct, according to the rules he had given, his church would be well provided for, as to its safety in these matters. And therefore those ministers of Christ and overseers of souls, that busy themselves, and are full of concern about the involuntary motions of the fluids and solids of men's bodies, and from thence full of doubts and suspicions of the cause, when nothing appears but that the state and frame of their minds, and their voluntary behavior is good, and agreeable to God's word; I say, such ministers go out of the place that Christ has set them in, and leave their proper business. . . .

3. Another thing that some make their rule to judge of this work by, instead of the Holy Scriptures, is history, or former observation. Herein they err two ways: *First,* if there be any

thing new and extraordinary in the circumstances of this work, that was not observed in former times, that is a rule with them to reject this work as not the work of God. Herein they make that their rule, that God has not given them for their rule; and limit God, where he has not limited himself. And this is especially unreasonable in this case: for whosoever has well weighed the wonderful and mysterious methods of divine wisdom, in carrying on the work of the new creation, or in the progress of the work of redemption, from the first promise of the seed of the woman to this time, may easily observe that it has all along been God's manner to open new scenes, and to bring forth to view things new and wonderful, such as eye had not seen, nor ear heard, nor entered into the heart of man or angels, to the astonishment of heaven and earth, not only in the revelations he makes of his mind and will, but also in the works of his hands. . . .

It is not unlikely that this work of God's spirit, that is so extraordinary and wonderful, is the dawning, or at least, a prelude of that glorious work of God, so often foretold in Scripture, which in the progress and issue of it shall renew the world of mankind. If we consider how long since, the things foretold, as what should precede this great event have been accomplished; and how long this event has been expected by the church of God, and thought to be nigh by the most eminent men of God in the church; and withal consider what the state of things now is, and has for a considerable time been, in the church of God, and world of mankind, we cannot reasonably think otherwise, than that the beginning of this great work of God must be near. And there are many things that make it probable that this work will begin in America. It is signified that it shall begin in some very remote part of the world, that the rest of the world will have no communication with but by navigation, in Isa. lx. 9: "Surely the Isles will wait for me, and the ships of Tarshish first, to bring my sons from afar." It is exceeding manifest that this chapter is a prophecy of the prosperity of the church, in its most glorious state on earth, in the latter days; and I cannot think that any thing else can here be intended but America, by the isles that are afar off, from whence the first born sons of that glorious day shall be brought. . . .

God has made as it were two worlds here below, the old and the new (according to the names they are now called by), two great habitable continents, far separated one from the other; the latter is but newly discovered, it was formerly wholly unknown, from age to age, and is as it were now but newly created: it has been, until of late, wholly the possession of Satan, the church of God having never been in it, as it has been in the other continent, from the beginning of the world. This new world is probably now discovered, that the new and most glorious state of God's church on earth might commence there; that God might in it begin a new world in a spiritual respect, when he creates the *new heavens* and *new earth.*

God has already put that honor upon the other continent, that Christ was born there literally, and there made the *purchase of redemption:* so, as Providence observes a kind of equal distribution of things, it is not unlikely that the great spiritual birth of Christ, and the most glorious *application of redemption* is to begin in this. . . .

The other continent hath slain Christ, and has from age to age shed the blood of the saints and martyrs of Jesus, and has often been as it were deluged with the church's blood: God has therefore probably reserved the honor of building the glorious temple to the daughter, that has not shed so much blood, when those times of the peace, and prosperity, and glory of the church shall commence, that were typified by the reign of Solomon. . . .

The old continent has been the source and original of mankind in several respects. The first parents of mankind dwelt there; and there dwelt Noah and his sons; and there the second Adam was born, and was crucified and rose again: and it is probable that, in some measure to balance these things, the most glorious renovation of the world shall originate from the new continent, and the church of God in that respect be from hence. And so it is probable that that will come to pass in spirituals, that has in temporals, with respect to America; that whereas till of late, the world was supplied with its silver and gold and earthly treasures from the old continent, now it is supplied chiefly from the new, so the course of things in spiritual respects will be in like manner turned.

And it is worthy to be noted that America was discovered about the time of the reformation, or but little before: which reformation was the first thing that God did towards the glorious renovation of the world, after it had sunk into the depths of darkness and ruin, under the great antichristian apostasy. So that as soon as this new world is (as it were) created, and stands forth in view, God presently goes about doing some great thing to make way for the introduction of the church's latter day glory, that is to have its first seat in, and is to take its rise from that new world.

It is agreeable to God's manner of working, when he accomplishes any glorious work in the world, to introduce a new and more excellent state of his church, to begin his work where his church had not been till then, and where was no foundation already laid, that the power of God might be the more conspicuous; that the work migh appear to be entirely God's, and be more manifestly a creation out of nothing; agreeably to Hos. i. 10: "And it shall come to pass that in the place where it was said unto them, ye are not my people, there it shall be said unto them, ye are the sons of the living God." When God is about to turn the earth into a Paradise, he does not begin his work where there is some good growth already, but in a wilderness, where nothing grows, and nothing is to be seen but dry sand and barren rocks; that the light may shine out of darkness, and the world be replenished from emptiness and the earth watered by springs from a droughty desert; agreeably to many prophecies of Scripture. . . .

I observed before, that when God is about do some great work for his church, his manner is to begin at the lower end; so when he is about to renew the whole habitable earth, it is probable that he will begin in this utmost, meanest, youngest and weakest part of it, where the church of God has been planted last of all; and so the first shall be last, and the last first; and that will be fulfilled in an eminent manner in Isa. xxiv. 16, "From the uttermost part of the earth have we heard songs, even glory to the righteous". . . .

And if we may suppose that this glorious work of God shall begin in any part of America, I think if we consider the circumstances of the settlement of New England, it must needs appear the most likely of all American colonies, to be the place whence this work shall principally take its rise.

And if these things are so, it gives more abundant reason to hope that what is now seen in America, and especially in New England, may prove the dawn of that glorious day: and the very uncommon and wonderful circumstances and events of this work, seem to me strongly to argue that God intends it as the beginning or forerunner of something vastly great.

I have thus long insisted on this point, because if these things are so, it greatly manifests how much it behooves us to encourage and promote this work, and how dangerous it will be to forbear so to do.

PART TWO
Exegesis

16 Edwin S. Gaustad
A Great and General Awakening

*Where and to what extent did the Awakening touch the people?
Over time the answer has been diverse. Prompted in particular by an
article by historian John C. Miller ("Religion, Finance, and Democracy
in Massachusetts," New England Quarterly, VI, 1933), which put forth
the thesis that the Awakening involved primarily the lower degrees of
New England's society and that it tended to exacerbate class conflict,
Edwin S. Gaustad argued in 1954 that it was all-pervasive, at least in
its first shock. Gaustad was at the time completing what is still a
standard work on the New England revival—The Great Awakening in
New England (New York, 1957). His answer to the question has not
as yet been directly challenged.*

Contemporaries of the turbulent religious upheaval which took
place in New England in the years 1740 to 1742 described it
as a "great and general awakening." Later historians, less ready
to admit either its greatness or its generality, have in concert
described the revival as limited to this area or that, to this
social class exclusive of that, and as brought about by this or
that socio-economic force. We have come a long way from "the
economic interpretation of religion," when all felt obliged to ex-
cuse the obtrusion of churches and pious sentiments by explain-
ing that this sheep's clothing of religion concealed an economic
wolf within. Yet the phenomenon known as the Great Awakening is of such proportions as to lead to its interpretation as
something other than a religious movement.

It would be folly to suggest that the Awakening was completely divorced from the culture of eighteenth-century New

SOURCE. Edwin S. Gaustad, "Society and the Great Awakening in New
England," *William and Mary Quarterly*, Ser. 3, XI (1954), pp. 566–577.
Reprinted by permission of the Institute of Early American History and
Culture and the author.

England, from the shortage of specie, from the growth of trade,
from the greater leisure and less crudity of life, from the vigilant
struggles for popular representation and the increasing degree of
political independence. To admit its connection with these secular developments is, however, vastly different from cataloguing
the revival as a "deep-rooted social movement," as a lower-class
uprising, or as "a revolt of the backcountry producers." John
Chester Miller viewed the movement as riding on the wave of
hostility between rich and poor created by the Land Bank up-
roar, and producing a full and permanent cleavage between the
social classes. The uninhibited and fervent James Davenport,
according to Miller, divided the

"social classes much as during the Land Bank fervor. The Opposers were joined by more and more of the wealthy and educated as Davenport carried the Great Awakening down to a lower
stratum and preached the gospel of discontent and levellism. . . .
This conviction among the common people that they had been
singled out by God for salvation and that the Opposers—the
upper classes—were for the most part damned gave class feelings
a new twist in Massachusetts."

Though this theory probably serves as a useful counterweight
to that other tenacious myth that "the elect" and "the elite"
were synonymous terms in colonial New England, it does not do
justice to the historical evidence concerning the revival itself.
Indeed, John Miller begins his discussion with a question that
begs the question: "What caused the Great Awakening to split
up the Congregational church and cut a swath between rich and
poor, stimulating the hostility that already divided them?" This
identification of the anti-revivalists with the upper classes is
made by Perry Miller, who declares the list of subscribers to
Chauncy's *Seasonable Thoughts* to be "a roster of antirevivalists
and also a social register." Eugene E. White writes of the revival
as one of the "deep-rooted social movements," a "social phenomenon," "confined to the cities and the settled areas of the
East." More recently, Richard D. Mosier views it as an affair
not of the cities, but of the rural areas, "a revolt of the back-

country producers from the stringent controls of the mercantile aristocracy which ruled from afar;" the Awakening was also anti-clerical and anarchical, "the first step in a movement which culminates in the American Revolution." And Clinton Rossiter, speaking of the Great Awakening in all the colonies, writes as follows: "It appealed primarily to the poor and despised; it revolted the well-born, well-educated, and well-to-do." These are statements of faith.[1]

There is, on the contrary, abundant evidence that this religious turmoil was in fact "great and general," that it knew no boundaries, social or geographical, that it was both urban and rural, that it reached both lower and upper class. The geographical non-particularity of the Great Awakening is readily established, though it is necessary to distinguish it from the earlier series of revivals emanating from Northampton. Beginning in 1734 and continuing for two or three years, these revivals were largely a frontier phenomenon, concentrated along the banks of the Connecticut River from Northfield to Saybrook Point. They arose under the influence of Jonathan Edwards and the "surprising conversions" which took place in Northampton. To them, but only to them, the term "frontier revivalism" can with propriety be applied, and not to the Great Awakening, which began after the earlier revivals were "very much at a Stop" and the initial phase of which occurred rather in the coastal than in the inland area. Edwards regarded the two movements as quite distinct, speaking of the revivalism early in 1741 as "the beginning of that extraordinary religious commotion, through the land. . . ." In the frontier revivals, no churches were split, no clergy were offended, no flagrant itineracy occurred, no elaborate apologetic was necessary, no legislation was provoked, and no vast array of abusive epithets came into use.

The Awakening itself began when, on September 14, 1740, the proud, portly, and pompous George Whitefield arrived at

---

[1] Quoted from John C. Miller, cited in the headnote; Perry Miller, *Jonathan Edwards* (New York, 1949) ; White, "Decline of the Great Awakening in New England: 1741 to 1746," *New England Quarterly*, XXIV (1951); Mosier, *The American Temper* (Berkeley, 1952) ; and Rossiter, *Seedtime of the Republic* (New York, 1953) .

Newport to preach (he tells us) with "much Flame, Clearness
and Power. . . . The People were exceedingly attentive. Tears
trickled down their Cheeks. . . ." His arrogance passed for conviction, his sentiment for piety, his superficiality for simplicity,
and his moving rhetoric for inspiration. And wherever the youth-
ful Anglican went, so did the Awakening. It spread from Newport to Bristol to Boston, and northeast to Roxbury, Marblehead,
Ipswich, Newbury, Hampton, Portsmouth, and York. It moved
west of Boston into Concord, Sudbury, Worcester, Leicester,
Brookfield, and Northampton; thence south, through Springfield,
Suffield, Windsor, Hartford, and New Haven; and southwest,
through Milford, Stratford, Fairfield, and Stamford. In less than
two months, the tour of New England by "the Grand Itinerant"
was over. From the many areas left shaking, tremors reached
out to meet each other, and to move all that lay between.

At the small town of Harvard, about forty miles west of Boston, "God was pleased . . . to rouze and awaken sleepy Sinners," this being done without the intervention of any itinerants
or "Strangers." On November 23, 1741, all heaven broke loose
in Middleborough, Massachusetts. "I have written Accounts of
seventy-six that Day struck, and bro't first to inquire what they
should do to escape condemnation." Their joyful pastor, Peter
Thacher, further notes that from that time on, there was "an
uncommon Teachableness among my People." In Weathersfield,
Connecticut, Eleazar Wheelock reported late in 1741 that "the
Lord bowed the heavens and Came Down upon a Large assembly in one of the Parishes of the town the Whole assembly
Seam'd alive with Distress. . . ." Gilbert Tennent, who followed
Whitefield in a tour of New England, observed that at Charlestown "multitudes were awakened, and several had received great
consolation, especially among the young people, children and
Negroes." He recorded also a general "shaking among the dry
bones" at Harvard College, while in New Haven the concern
was considerable and "about thirty students came on foot ten
miles to hear the word of God." In brief, it is simply not possible to draw any meaningful lines on a map of New England in
order to distinguish where in 1741 the revival was and where it
was not. It was a phenomenon not alone of the back country or

exclusively of the cities, of the coast or of the frontier. From Stamford, Connecticut, to York, Maine, from Danbury to Northfield (the New England Dan to Beersheba), there had been a great and general awakening.

In 1742, six Boston ministers testified that these "uncommon religious Appearances" were found "among Persons of all Ages and Characters." Another Boston clergyman, the fiery Presbyterian John Moorhead, extolled "the wonderful things which God is adoing, and has already Manifested amongst Indians, Negros, Papists and Protestants of all Denominations." Though somewhat extreme, Moorhead's observation points to the truly universal character of the Awakening. If it reached Indians, Negroes, and even Quakers, is it possible that it extended also to the upper classes?

It has never seemed urgently necessary to offer proof of lower-class participation in the revival, perhaps because of the finality of such a quotation as the following, which describes James Davenport and his Boston listeners:

"Were you to see him in his most violent agitations, you would be apt to think, that he was a Madman just broke from his Chains: But especially had you seen him returning from the Common after his first preaching, with a large Mob at his Heels, singing all the Way thro' the Streets . . . attended with so much Disorder, that they look'd more like a Company of Bacchanalians after a mad Frolick, than sober Christians who had been worshipping God. . . ."

A strong image such as this lingers long in the imagination, causing Davenport and his large mob, in retrospect, to seem the epitome of the Awakening. Even in those surveys of New England's revival where Davenport is not regarded as its personification, he is given disproportionate emphasis. There was no Davenport party. By the ardent supporters of the revival he was judged, in the middle of 1742, to be "deeply tinctur'd with a Spirit of Enthusiasm," and unworthy to be invited "into our Places of publick Worship"—this from the ministers who diligently worked in behalf of the "great and glorious work of God."

Indeed, the friends of the Awakening feared him more than its foes, for they recognized in him the potential for discrediting the entire movement. Thomas Prince, joyfully describing the successes of the revival in Boston, tells of Davenport's coming in these words: "And then through the providence of the sovereign God, the wisdom of whose ways are past finding out, we unexpectedly came to an unhappy period, which it exceedingly grieves me now to write of. . . ." His fellow Presbyterian, Gilbert Tennent, himself repeatedly condemned for going to rash and intemperate extremes, denounced Davenport's technique as "enthusiastical, proud, and schismatical." Further, in the summer of 1742, a Connecticut court found Davenport "disturbed in the rational Faculties of his Mind," while a Massachusetts court declared him *non compos mentis*. To be sure, if Davenport represented anything at all, it would be of a lower order. The point is, however, that he was the spokesman for no class or party, and least of all is he a symbol of the Great Awakening as a whole.

When Whitefield departed from Boston on his first New England tour, the *Evening-Post* editorialized that "the Town is in a hopeful way of being restor'd to its former State of Order, Peace and Industry." Three days later, a letter, appearing in the *News-Letter,* deplored this attitude, affirming that "the Generality of sober and serious Persons, of all Denominations among us (who perhaps are as much for maintaining Order, Peace and Industry as Mr. Evening-Post and Company) have been greatly Affected with Mr. Whitefield's Plain, Powerful, and Awakening Preaching. . . ." Were the "sober and serious" actually reached by the revival? Benjamin Colman, of the Brattle Street Church, wrote Whitefield that after Tennent's visit to Boston "great Additions are made to our Churches. . . . Many of them among the Rich and Polite of our Sons and Daughters. This week the overseers of our Colleges have appointed a Day of Prayer and Humiliation with thanksgiving, for the Effusion of the Spirit of God. . . ." The phrase, "especially among young people," often occurs in contemporary accounts of the revival, suggesting a greater concentration of "concern" in that generation. But that the movement followed class lines, there is no indication.

With reference to the colleges, of which Colman spoke and of whose social standing there can be little question, their sympathies would have remained with the Awakening had not Whitefield heedlessly insulted them. Yale and Harvard both cheerfully heard the leading exponents of the movement, and some of the instructional staff left their posts to carry the word. An effective deterrent to their support was this remark, published in Whitefield's *Journal:* "As for the Universities, I believe it may be said, their Light is become Darkness, Darkness that may be felt, and is complained of by the most godly Ministers." Whitefield sought to mitigate the effect of this unwarranted affront by writing a letter in July, 1741, "To the Students, &c. under convictions at the colleges of Cambridge and New-Haven," declaring that "It was no small grief to me, that I was obliged to say of your college, that 'your light was become darkness;' yet are ye now become light in the Lord." The damage had already been done; nevertheless, not until 1744 did Harvard issue a formal testimony against Whitefield, Yale following suit in 1745. Even then, it must be noted, the testimony was "Against the Reverend Mr. George Whitefield, And his Conduct" and not against the revival in general. Yale and Harvard graduates alike continued to bear the main responsibility in furthering the "extraordinary Work of God."

Pro-revivalism was in no way the equivalent of social egalitarianism. One of the sins for which Jonathan Edwards reproved his young people was their spending much time in "frolicks," without having "any regard to order in the families they belonged to. . . ." There was a large measure of social consciousness in Edwards's Northampton parish, as later events even more clearly revealed; yet the church could hardly be regarded as outside the scope of the Awakening. Ebenezer Parkman of Westborough, a peerless social conservative, was fully sympathetic with the revival at the same time that he complained in horror that the young men of the lower classes had the presumption to adorn themselves with "Velvet Whoods." Gilbert Tennent, often represented as a leveller and "a Man of no great Parts or Learning," had in fact received from his father no mean education in Hebrew, the classics, and theology, and could move easily in any stratum of society.

In Boston, then if not now, the upper reaches of New England society were concentrated. And that city's support of the revival was an effective force in the entire movement. When Whitefield first came to town, he was "met on the Road and conducted to Town by several Gentlemen." Later in the week, he dined with the governor, Jonathan Belcher, with whom he enjoyed a most cordial relationship. Of Boston's four newspapers, three were either favorable to the Awakening or successfully maintained some degree of neutrality. Only Timothy Fleet's rather coarse *Evening-Post* was openly opposed to the revival, and even this paper did not dare to swim against the tide of public feeling until near the end of 1742, when the movement had already begun to ebb.

The established clergy of New England's capital were preponderantly pro-revivalist or New Light: the proportion was three to one. Of the three divines hostile to the Great Awakening, only Charles Chauncy was open and active in his opposition, and he did not begin a deliberate refutation of the revival until 1743. Throughout 1741, Chauncy allowed himself to be carried along in the main current of the movement, even to the point of telling sinners that they "hang, as it were, over the bottomless pit, by the slender thread of life, and the moment that snaps asunder, you sink down into perdition. . . ." As late as May of 1742, Chauncy declared, "There are, I doubt not, a number in this land, upon whom God has graciously shed the influence of his blessed Spirit. . . ." So that during the height of the Awakening, 1740 to 1742, its most able and prodigious opponent sounded much like Jonathan Edwards himself. The two remaining Old Lights or "Opposers" among Boston's established clergy, both of the Mather family, published nothing concerning the religious excitement, though they privately expressed their disdain of the affair. Samuel Mather, son of Cotton, was dismissed from Second Church in 1741 because, among other reasons, of his negative attitude toward the Awakening and his reluctance to participate in it. In a vain attempt at reconciliation, Mather promised "to beware of any thing in my sermons or conversation which may tend to discourage the work of conviction and conversion among us." Mather Byles, grandson of Increase and first pastor of the Hollis Street Church, succeeded in avoiding any public controversy over the revival. Though publishing a sermon in 1741 on *Repentance and Faith The Great Doctrine of the Gospel of Universal Concernment,* Byles' position—religious and political—was unalterably conservative, and his sympathies were thoroughly Old Light.

Except for three wavering neutrals, the other Boston ministers vigorously, tirelessly, promoted the revival. The city's senior pastor at this time was Benjamin Colman, of Brattle Street Church. A great friend to institutions of higher learning and widely respected abroad as well as at home for his erudition, Colman received the degree of Doctor of Divinity in 1731 from the University of Glasgow. Liberal and learned, he did not hesitate to "play the Artillery of Heaven against the hardy Sons of Vice," and in 1741 he happily reported that "The Work of God with us goes on greatly . . . our crowded serious Assemblies continue, and great Additions are made to our Churches." Following Whitefield's initial visit, Colman spoke at Boston's first evening lecture of the pleasure it gave the ministers to see "in the Weeks past, Old and Young, Parents and Children, Masters and Servants, high and low, rich and poor together, gathering . . . to the Doors and Windows of our Places of Worship. . . ." Benjamin Colman is certainly to be regarded as a constant friend of the Awakening—though, just as certainly, he is to be distinguished from such fanatics as James Davenport and Andrew Croswell. His position, however, was rather one of discrimination than of moderation. He had even shown great interest in the earlier Northampton revival, corresponding with Edwards and others connected with it, passing on to his friends abroad news of religious awakenings in the colonies, and urging Edwards to write the *Faithful Narrative of Surprising Conversions.* The first minister of New England to correspond with Whitefield, he was instrumental in bringing the latter to that area. With much zeal and sincere concern, he favored and furthered

the revival to the very end, seeking, like Edwards, to discourage
the excesses and abnormalities as no proper part of the true display of God's grace.

William Cooper, Colman's associate since 1715, joined with
his colleague in praising "the remarkable Work of Grace begun, and I hope going on amongst us; the eminent Success which
God has been pleas'd to give to his preached Gospel of late;
the surprizing Effusion of the Holy Spirit, as a Spirit of Conversion to a blessed Number. . . ." At First Church, there was
no such harmony. Chauncy's opposition was offset by the approbation of his associate, Thomas Foxcroft, of what he called
the "Pauline Spirit and Doctrine remarkably exemplify'd among
us." Thomas Prince and Joseph Sewall of Old South Church
were eminently successful in making that church a vital center of
revival activity. Prince, Boston's foremost reporter of the Awakening, was largely responsible for the creation of the disorganized
but important *Christian History,* the first specifically religious
magazine in the colonies, the purpose of which was to give
accounts of the "surprizing and . . . extensive Revivals." Although it was ostensibly edited by Thomas Prince, Junior, the
magazine's enemies were probably correct in declaring the elder
Prince to be the power behind the pen. Joseph Sewall, who
looked upon the revival as itself a means or channel of grace,
inveighed against "every Thing that hath a Tendency to quench
his [God's] Spirit, and obstruct the Progress and Success of his
good Work." John Webb, senior minister at New North Church,
vividly portrayed Christ entreating reluctant sinners in this time
of concern to seek and receive the saving grace. His colleague,
Andrew Eliot, in 1743 signed a testimony favoring the Great
Awakening, noting only that itineracy had not been sufficiently
protested against. Samuel Checkley of New South Church, who
in 1741 preached on the topic "Little children brought to Christ,"
was among the same group of signers. And Joshue Gee of Second Church, having reproved the cool indifference of his associate, Samuel Mather, exploded with bitterness when in 1743
a group of ministers issued a testimony against errors and disorders in the Awakening without making "an open Acknowledgement of the late remarkable Effects of a gracious Divine In-

fluence in many of our Churches." Gee succeeded in calling a gathering of ninety New England ministers who were "persuaded there has of late been a happy Revival of Religion," and in issuing a favorable witness to the revival signed by sixty-eight divines and attested to by forty-three others unable to attend the meeting.

The division of Boston's Congregational clergy in this turbulent period is, therefore, as follows: nine New Light, three Old Light, three neutral. Five churches were pro-revivalist (Brattle Street, Old South, Second, New North, and New South) ; New Brick and West were neutral; Hollis Street was anti-revivalist; and First was divided. The city's one Presbyterian church, with John Moorhead as pastor, was as determined in its support of the Awakening as the one Baptist church was in its opposition. One segment of Boston society did hold aloof: namely, that which attended the city's three Anglican churches. But respectability, in eighteenth-century New England at least, was not wholly identified with Anglicanism. Even as it is impossible to fix any meaningful geographical boundaries to the sweep of the Awakening, so the attempt to limit its sway or ascribe its rise to any single social class proves misleading.

As the revival declined and the "distinguishing names of reproach" came to be employed more freely and less gently, theological and ecclesiastical factions hardened, sometimes producing divisions that were social—in Connecticut, even political. With the increase in animosities, reports of revivalism were dismissed as "stupid Bombast Stuff," and Ezra Stiles in 1760 described the period of the revival as a time when "Multitudes were seriously, soberly and solemnly out of their wits." A Connecticut divine summarized the effects of the movement as follows:

"Antinomian Principles are advanc'd, preach'd up and printed;—Christian Brethren have their Affections widely alienated;—Unchristian Censoriousness and hard judging abounds, Love stands afar of, and Charity cannot enter;—Many Churches and Societies are broken and divided. . . . Numbers of illiterate Exhorters swarm about as Locusts from the Bottomless Pit. . . ."

As such reports came to abound, it seemed plausible, if not
desirable, to describe the revival as socially suspect from the
beginning, as carried along by a disinherited, rural debtor class.
It is, however, tendentious history that sees New England's religious upheaval of 1740 to 1742 as something less than "a
great and general awakening."

17 FROM *Vernon L. Parrington*
An Anachronism in the Age of Reason

*Vernon Louis Parrington, for a long time Professor of English at
the University of Washington prior to his death in 1929, and author
of the three-volume* Main Currents in American Thought *(New York,
1927–30), reflected and propagated the almost classic view of the
Awakening. Calvinism was dying—as it had to if democratic and liberal
America was to come into being; Jonathan Edwards was the "reactionary Calvinist" who attempted to revive the moribund; so too, by
implication, were the awakeners in general. And if these reactionaries,
by their awakening, set off "a little revolution" in the sense of the
break-up of the traditional order, it was mere irony to Parrington.
They were anachronisms, harking back to the past, while their enemies
among the rationalists (Chauncy, for example) were making the American mind.*

Before an adequate democratic philosophy could arise in this
world of pragmatic individualism, the traditional system of New
England theology must be put away, and a new conception of
man and of his duty and destiny in the world must take its
place. For the moment Calvinism was strengthened by the com-

SOURCE. Vernon L. Parrington, *Main Currents in American Thought,*
Volume I, *The Colonial Mind, 1620–1800,* New York: Harcourt, Brace &
World, Inc., 1927 (renewed, 1955, by Vernon L. Parrington, Jr., Louise P.
Tucker, and Elizabeth P. Thomas), pp. 148–152, 159–162. Reprinted by
permission of Harcourt, Brace & World, Inc.

ing of the Scotch-Irish who spread the familiar dogmas along the frontier, remote from attack by old-world rationalism; nevertheless those dogmas carried with them the seeds of slow decay. The world that had created them lay in a forgotten past. The five points of Calvinism, postulated on a God of wrath, were no longer living principles answering to common experience; they were become no other than ghosts that walked on the Sabbath to terrify the timid. An intellectual *Aufklarung* was a necessary preliminary to the creation of a fruitful social philosophy. Theology must be made to square with actuality, or yield control of men's minds to more stimulating things.

But unfortunately there was no vigorous attack but only a tedious decay. The old was too deeply entrenched to be routed, and stricken with palsy it lingered out a morose old age. For years New England stewed in its petty provincialism, untouched by the brisk debates that stirred the old world. No vigorous disputant challenged its orthodoxy. In the year 1726 Cotton Mather wrote, "I cannot learn, That among all the Pastors of Two Hundred Churches, there is one Arminian; much less an Arian, or a Gentilist." Nevertheless rationalism was in the air, and although it might be excluded from the minister's study, it spread its subtle infection through the mass of the people. The backwash of English deism reached the shores of New England, and by the decade of the forties a movement of liberalism seems to have got under way. The word Arminian sprinkles more freely the pages of controversial literature, indicating the nature of the attack being directed against Calvinism. Dogma was face to face with rationalism.

A critical movement had long been developing in England, undermining there the foundations of Calvinism; and in this work members of the Anglican clergy had aided. Hooker[2] had been a rationalist and the influence of the *Ecclesiastical Polity* was thrown in favor of an appeal to reason and to history. He rejected a literal Hebraism for a more philosophical interpretation of the Scripture. "The Light of naturall understanding, wit

---

[2] Richard Hooker, a late sixteenth and early seventeenth-century divine whose works strongly influenced Anglican doctrine.

and reason, is from God," he argued; "he it is which thereby doth illuminate every man entering into the World. He is the Author of all that we think or do by vertue of that light which himselfe hath given." Because of this rationalizing tendency the Anglican clergy, before the middle of the seventeenth century, had passed from the Calvinistic to the Arminian position. The fundamental dogma of Arminianism was the doctrine of the freedom of the will—that the elect of God are not pre-chosen, but a righteous life and good works will bring men into the way of salvation. Destructive of the whole Calvinistic system as such doctrine was—striking at the taproot of determinism—Arminianism carried a social significance greater than its theological import: it was an expression of the ideal of individual responsibility that emerged from the decay of the feudal system. The first reformers had asserted the right to individual interpretation of the Scriptures; the Arminians threw upon the individual the whole responsibility, bidding him assert his will and achieve his own salvation.

English rationalism was carried further by a notable group of thinkers . . . who rapidly passed from Arminianism to Arianism, and thence to deism. By the beginning of the eighteenth century English Presbyterianism, which had clung to Calvinism long after the defection of the Anglicans, was undermined by the growing rationalism and finally passed over into Unitarianism. Calvinism had lost the battle in the old world and ceased to play an important part in the intellectual life of England. In the face of this steady drift away from the conception of a divine Will that dwarfed the human will and held it fixed in the mesh of the divine purpose, towards the conception of the responsibility of the individual and the significance of the moral code in the work of salvation, the New England Calvinists found their work cut out for them. A critical spirit was stirring, an incipient rationalism was beginning to ask questions; orthodoxy for the first time was on the defensive, and ill equipped for the pending battle.

But Calvinism had fallen into the clutch of forces greater and more revolutionary than either minister or congregation realized. To preach with convincing force one must appeal to the common experience; dogma must seem to square with the evident facts of life; it must appear to be the inevitable and sufficient explanation of the mysteries and perplexities that beset men in the world of reality. When it ceases to be a reasonable working hypothesis in the light of common experience, it is no longer a controlling influence in men's lives. And this was the unhappy predicament in which Calvinism now found itself. Take, for example, the doctrine of total depravity. In the corrupt worlds of Augustine and John Calvin such a doctrine must have seemed a reasonable explanation of the common brutality; an evil society must spring from the evil heart of man. But in the village world of New England the doctrine had lost its social sanction. When in moments of calm sense these provincial Calvinists asked themselves if the human heart were in truth utterly depraved, if they themselves and their neighbors were such vipers and worms as they professed to be, the conviction must have grown upon them that such professions were untrue. The everyday life of the New England village was animated by rugged virtues—by kindliness towards neighbors and faithfulness to a strict ethical code, rather than by hatred to God and man, or brutal wallowing in sin. In short, these villagers knew that they were very far from a bad lot; and when they pondered on this fact they must have discovered increasing difficulty in reconciling Sunday dogma and weekday experience. Although they repeated the familiar creed, the sanction for that creed was gone; it was the voice of dogma that spoke, and not the voice of reason and experience.

Such is the explanation, as well, of the decay of another of the cardinal points of Calvinism—the dogma of special election. In an aristocratic society it is natural to believe that God has set men apart in classes; but as the leveling process tended to strip away social distinctions, the new individualism undermined the older class psychology. When the common man has freed himself from political absolutism, he will become dissatisfied with theological absolutism. The right to achieve salvation is a natural corollary to the right to win social distinction; that one's future status lay wholly beyond the reach of one's will, that it rested in the hands of an arbitrary God who gave or withheld salvation at pleasure, was a conception that ill accorded with the nascent ideal of democracy. When that ideal should be sufficiently clarified, the dogma of the elect of God, like the aristocratic conception of the king's favorite, would be quietly put away in the potter's field.

As the century advanced, the growing dissatisfaction with Calvinism received fresh impetus from the new social philosophy of France. The teaching of Rousseau that in a state of nature men were good, that they are still sound at heart, and that the evils of civilization have resulted from a perversion of the social contract, would appeal to men whose experience was daily teaching them the falseness of the traditional dogmas; and the ideal of equality would come home with special meaning to men bred up in villages and on the frontier. Such doctrines were fundamentally hostile to the spirit of Calvinism: not only did Rousseau set the doctrine of human perfectibility over against the dogma of total depravity, but he quickened the passion of revolt against every form of arbitrary authority, theological as well as political and social. Although the provincial colonial might not come in immediate contact with such speculative philosophy, in the long run he could not escape being influenced by it, and that influence would count against a decadent theology that held men's minds in its tenacious *rigor mortis*.

The crux of the question, it came finally to be seen by the apologists of the old order, lay in the fundamental problem of determinism. Was the will of man effectively free, or was it held in strict subjection to the stable will of God? According as the decision went touching this question, would stand or fall the entire metaphysical structure of Calvinism. To this problem, therefore, the best minds among the ministers directed their thought; and the historical position of Jonathan Edwards, greatest of the defenders of Calvinism, is revealed in its true perspective when his labors are studied in the light of this vital question. . . .

Under the rod of [his] logic—grotesque, abortive, unseasoned by any saving knowledge of human nature—Edwards preached that remarkable series of imprecatory sermons that sank deep into the memory of New England, and for which it has never forgiven him. Unfortunate as those sermons were in darkening the fame of an acute thinker, disastrous as they were in providing a sanction for other men to terrify the imaginations of ill-balanced persons, we cannot regret that Edwards devoted his logic to an assidious stoking of the fires of hell. The theology of Calvin lay like a heavy weight upon the soul of New England, and there could be no surer way to bring it into disrepute, than to thrust into naked relief the brutal grotesqueries of those dogmas that professed thus to explain the dark mysteries which lie upon the horizons of life. For a long while yet they were to harass the imagination of New England, but the end already could be foreseen. Once the horrors that lay in the background of Calvinism were disclosed to common view, the system was doomed. It might still wear the semblance of life; it might still remain as an evil genius to darken the conscience of men and women; but its authoritative appeal was gone. In this necessary work of freeing the spirit of New England, no other thinker played so large or so unconscious a part as Jonathan Edwards; and it was the notorious minatory sermons—the translation into vivid images of the generalized dogmas—that awakened the popular mind to an understanding of the conclusions involved in the premises.

While Edwards was thus hastening the decay of Calvinism with his lurid painting of "the landscape of hell," in another phase of his work he was engaged in awakening an interest in religion among the slothful churches. He had long been interested in the phenomena of conversion, and as the great revival of the forties, led by Whitefield, spread from England to the colonies, he joined eagerly in the work. In consequence of an earlier revival in his parish of Northampton, his attention had been drawn to the little understood psychology of the awakening soul, and with the detachment of the scientist he set himself to study the problem. The terrors aroused by his minatory sermons provided his clinical laboratory with numerous cases of abnormal emotionalism. Day after day he probed and analyzed and compared, until as a result of his close studies in vivisection, he became a specialist in the theory of conversion, commanding the eager attention of a generation that had come to look upon this as the central fact of Christian experience. It is not easy today to be sympathetic with this phase of Edwards's work; it belongs equally with his dogmas to a world of thought that is no longer ours. The repulsive records as they are set down in his *Narrative of the Surprizing Works of God,* marked by evidence of pathological states of mind not far removed from insanity, no longer seem a testimony to God's beneficent presence; the spiritual writhings which this gentle-natured student watched with such fascination, appear rather to be cases for the alienist to prescribe for. But to Edwards the terrors of a five-year-old girl were not pathological; they were the soul-labors of the spiritual rebirth, the visible signs of the supreme miracle of the universe, filling him with wonder and awe at God's infinite mercy; and like a modern psychologist he was at enormous pains to chart the successive steps in the miraculous transformation.

Other and greater consequences were to flow from the new revivalism. The Great Awakening was the single movement that stirred the colonial heart deeply during three generations. It reveals, among other things, that America was still living in the world of the seventeenth century: that the upper class was not yet rationalized, nor the middle class commercialized. Theology was still of greater popular interest than politics. In its chief phenomena the Great Awakening was a return to an earlier age—to those unbalanced enthusiasms of the Puritan upheaval. It was essentially a mass movement. Its use of hypnotic suggestion, its lurid terrorism, its outcries and hysterical possessions, reveal like the Ranters of a hundred years before the phenomena of mob psychology, and it made appeal to the ill-educated, the isolated, the neurotic, to the many natural victims of hypnotic excitation bred by the monotony and austerity of village life. Its after effects were revolutionary, for the quickening of religious emotionalism marked the beginning of the end of Puritan formalism.

The bitter quarrel among the churches which followed as an aftermath was more than a theological dispute; it was a sign of the breaking up of the traditional parish system. The hierarchy had long before lost its authority, but in their several parishes the ministers still enjoyed patriarchal power. The tragic dismissal of Edwards from his parish was an unprecedented revolt against that authority. But greater changes were to follow. After the Great Awakening itinerant preachers made their appearance who presumed to enter any parish without the consent of the minister, and preach such doctrines as they would. They were non-conforming free lances, hostile to the established church, whose stock-in-trade was the new emotionalism. Under their leadership, Separatist congregations were gathered that were not only an offense to the regular establishment but a challenge to its authority. Hundreds left the old congregations and flocked to the Baptists and Methodists, and naturally they would make trouble over paying taxes to support a church they had repudiated. In short, a little revolution was under way that was to end in the complete disintegration of the parish system.

By a curious irony of fate, Jonathan Edwards, reactionary Calvinist and philosophical recluse, became the intellectual leader of the revolutionaries. His insistence upon conversion as the sole ground of admission to communion was the final blow that destroyed the old theocratic system which the Mathers had labored to uphold. Church and state were effectively cut asunder by such a test. There is no evidence that Edwards was concerned about the political or social consequences that must result from the abandonment of the traditional "Half-way Covenant."[3] It was a question of doctrine with him, involving only matters of church discipline. Although he was accused of being a Separatist, and of seeking to disintegrate the parish system, he had no thought of attacking a parochial order that he held in high esteem. He was unconcerned that his teachings led straight to the old Separatist conclusion that it is the church mystical which Christ established, and not the church visible. Nevertheless he became the creator of the new Congregationalism, which in accepting the democratic principles elaborated by John Wise and establishing the local church as an autonomous unit, effectively nullified the Presbyterian tendencies of the old order.

As one follows the laborious career of this great thinker, a sense of the tragic failure of his life deepens. The burdens that he assumed were beyond the strength of any man. Beginning as a mystic, brooding on the all-pervasive spirit of sweetness

---

[3] See below, Perry Miller on the halfway covenant.

and light diffused through the universe, with its promise of spiritual emancipation; then turning to an archaic theology and giving over his middle years to the work of minifying the excellence of man in order to exalt the sovereignty of God; and finally settling back upon the mystical doctrine of conversion— such a life leaves one with a feeling of futility, a sense of great powers baffled and wasted, a spiritual tragedy enacted within the narrow walls of a minister's study. There was both pathos and irony in the fate of Jonathan Edwards, removed from the familiar places where for twenty years he had labored, the tie with his congregation broken, and sent to the frontier mission at Stockbridge[4] to preach to a band of Indians and to speculate on the unfreedom of the human will. The greatest mind of New England had become an anachronism in a world that bred Benjamin Franklin.

[4] In 1750 Edwards was forced out of his Northampton pulpit; in 1751 he settled in Stockbridge, Mass., as an Indian missionary and pastor of an Indian-white church. He remained there until assuming the presidency of the College of New Jersey early in 1758.

18   FROM   H. Richard Niebuhr
Toward the Kingdom of God

In his several books, H. Richard Niebuhr—theologian, historian, and sociologist—has explored the interaction of religion and American society. To him, the Great Awakening was not in any way anachronistic. On the contrary, it was part of a steady conception of a divine will being acted out in America—one stretching from the very foundation of the colonies, through the Awakening and the reform and social gospel movements of the nineteenth century, to the present day, where it forms the core of America's secular idealism.

SOURCE. H. Richard Niebuhr, *The Kingdom of God in America*, New York: Harper & Row, Inc., 1937 (renewed, 1965, by Florence M. Niebuhr), pp. 135–150. Reprinted by permission of the publishers.

The Great Awakening and the revivals were ushered in by a new awareness of the coming kingdom. Edwards and Wesley,[5] like Paul and Luther before them, became intensely conscious of the great gap which exists between human performance and divine demand or between the actuality and the potentiality of human life. They saw a great opportunity and they strained all their efforts toward its realization. . . . The other leaders seem to have followed the same general pattern. Their hope was like that of their contemporaries; it was still the orthodox Western expectation of life in heaven. But they differed from others in the intensity of their anticipation. What to most men was an extra consolation and a supernatural addition to their expectations of success and joy on earth was very close, real and important to the embryonic Evangelicals. They felt keenly the wonder and the nearness of this possibility of life and, by the same token, the unsatisfactoriness of their present existence. They pressed therefore into the kingdom of God, as they understood that kingdom.

Their efforts failed—or, we may say, they were crowned with success as a result of failure. It became clear to them that though it was not possible for men to make the potential actual, yet what was impossible for men was both possible and actual for God. The idea of the coming kingdom came alive when it was connected with the conviction of God's living power. As the moralism of the Holy Club [of the Wesleys] was supplanted by the gospel of salvation so the Edwardean effort to progress toward the coming kingdom by self-discipline gave way to the recognition of divine sovereignty. Under these circumstances anticipations of the future became more rather than less intense. Now the coming kingdom appeared not as a goal toward which men were traveling but as the end which was hastening toward them; and now it was no longer simply the great happiness which men might miss but also the great threat which they could not escape. The new note was related to the old in the same way that communism in our time is related to utopian socialism.

[5] John Wesley, with his brother Charles, leader of the concurrent English revival.

The "hell-fire" sermons, which often seemed to be the only part of Edwards' preaching that later generations remembered, are profoundly misunderstood when they are taken out of their context in the theology of divine sovereignty and placed in the context of an institutionalism which used threats of hell like promises of heaven to frighten or to wheedle the immature into obedient acceptance of conventional piety and morality. Placed in their proper setting they represent Edwards' intense awareness of the precariousness of life's poise, of the utter insecurity of men and of mankind which are at every moment as ready to plunge into the abyss of disintegration, barbarism, crime and the war of all against all, as to advance toward harmony and integration. He recognized what Kierkegaard meant when he described life as treading water with ten thousand fathoms beneath us.

Man is preserved in his precarious balance, according to Edwards, only by the patience of God, in whose eyes the spawning, lusting, fighting, cruel life of humanity could scarcely be more lovely than insect existence is to men. "The God that holds you over the pit of hell, much as one holds a spider, or some loathsome insect over the fire, abhorrs you and is dreadfully provoked: his wrath toward you burns like fire, . . . he is of purer eyes than to bear to have you in his sight. . . . It is nothing but his hand that holds you from falling into the fire every moment."

What the prophets had realized was understood again by Edwards and his co-laborers: "Woe to you that desire the day of the Lord. The day of the Lord is darkness and not light." The coming kingdom understood as the apocalypse of the divine sovereignty was the fruition not only of divine goodness but of human badness in conflict with that unconquerable goodness. How much the Awakeners and revivers realized that the coming kingdom meant crisis as well as promise is evident from the titles of some of their sermons. Edwards preached not only on "Sinners in the Hand of an Angry God" but also on "Future Punishment of the Wicked Unavoidable and Intolerable," "The Eternity of Hell Torments," "The Final Judgment," "The Wicked Useful in their Destruction Only," "Wrath Upon the

Wicked to the Uttermost," "The End of the Wicked Contem-
plated by the Righteous." To these titles one may add Whitefield's "The Eternity of Hell Torments," Wesley's "The Great
Assize," "The Signs of the Times," "Of Hell," "On Redeeming
the Times" and many more similar subjects by their followers.
As for John the Baptist and the Jesus of the Synoptic Gospels,
the dramatic crisis of the impending future revealed to the
American disciples the actual crisis in the present. To be sure
the Evangelicals dealt with individual men who thought themselves secure in their isolation; they thought of the crisis in which
the individual stood and used death as the symbol in which the
threat to security became apparent, whereas the prophets of the
Old and New Testaments saw the crisis under the symbol of
social catastrophe. But in addressing individuals the Awakeners
dealt as faithfully with their own time as the prophets had done
with theirs. For judgment and death and the peril of falling
into a state of worthless existence belong to all things human.

The recognition that the coming kingdom of the divine sovereign meant destruction of much that men prized and that it
called for their immediate turning away from the ways that led
to darkness was only half of the Awakeners' gospel. The second element was good news. Beyond judgment lay the new
world of God, the kingdom of joy and peace, of unity and harmony, the realization of all the good potential in that human
life in which so much evil was also potential. The good news
was not only that there was light beyond darkness, but even
more that in Christ men had been given the opportunity to anticipate both threat and promise, to bring the future into the
present and to receive a foretaste of the coming kingdom, a
validation of the promise. John Woolman[6] offers as excellent
an illustration of the way in which the eighteenth century could
anticipate the coming kingdom as Paul does of the first century.
He wrote in his *Journal:*

"In a time of Sickness with plurisie a little upward of two
years and a half ago I was brought so Near the gates of death,

[6] A Quaker reformer and contemporary of Edwards.

that I forgot my name. Being then desirous to know who I was, I saw a mass of matter of a dully gloomy collour, between the South and the East, and was informed that this mass was human beings, in as great misery as they could be, & live, and that I was mixed in with them, & henceforth I might not consider myself as a distinct or Separate being. In this state I remained several hours. I then heard a soft melodious voice, more pure and harmonious than any voice I had heard with my ears before, and I believe it was the voice of an angel who spake to the other angels. The words were John Woolman is dead. I soon remembered that I once was John Woolman, and being assured that I was alive in the body, I greatly wondered what that heavenly voice could mean."

When "the mystery was opened" he "perceived there was Joy in heaven over a Sinner who had repented, and that that language, *John Woolman is dead,* meant no more than the death of my own will." The experiences of the thousands who met the crisis of life under the influences of Quaker and Evangelical preaching were doubtless usually less visionary, less complete and often less sincere. There are few Woolmans and Edwards' in any generation. Still, many experiences were genuine and through them American Christians in the eighteenth and early nineteenth centuries anticipated the coming kingdom by dying to self and rising with Christ.

The reality and the surprising scope of these experiences now brought a great surmise and hope to the leaders. What if this movement were itself the coming of the kingdom in power? It is remarkable how under the influence of the Great Awakening the millenarian expectation flourished in America. Hopkins[7] remarks that few writers in the seventeenth century said anything about this doctrine but "in the present century there has been more attention to it." To Edwards the surprising conversions indicated that "it is not unlikely that this work of God's Spirit, so extraordinary and wonderful, is the dawning, or at least a

---

[7] Samuel Hopkins, a major theologian of the late eighteenth century and an intimate of Edwards' during the latter's years at Stockbridge.

prelude of that glorious work of God, so often foretold in Scripture, which, in the progress and issue of it, shall renew the world of mankind." He gave various reasons why "we cannot reasonably think otherwise, than that the beginning of this great work of God must be near. And there are many things that make it probable that this work will begin in America." The Awakening appeared to him to be

"a great and wonderful event, a strange revolution, an unexpected surprising overturning of things, suddenly brought to pass. . . . It is the work of redemption (the great end of all the other works of God, and of which the work of creation was but a shadow) in the event, success, and end of it: It is the work of new creation which is infinitely more glorious than the old. . . . The New Jerusalem in this respect has begun to come down from heaven, and perhaps never were more of the prelibations of heaven's glory given upon earth."

In the *History of the Work of Redemption* and *An Humble Attempt to Promote Explicit Agreement and Visible Union of God's People in Extraordinary Prayers for the Revival of Religion* this millennial idea is developed. How the future revolution has been anticipated and the time foreshortened appears in this statement from the former work:

"The end of God's creating the world, was to prepare a kingdom for his Son . . . which should remain to all eternity. So far as the *kingdom of Christ* is set up in the world, *so far* is the world brought to its end, and the eternal state of things set up—*so far* are all the great changes and revolutions in the world brought to their everlasting issue, and all things come to their ultimate period. . . . So far as Christ's kingdom is established in the world, *so far* are things wound up and settled in their everlasting state, and a period put to the course of things in this changeable world, *so far* are the first heavens and the first earth come to an end, and the new heavens and the new earth, the everlasting heavens and earth established in their room."

Edwards believed that this *so far* must fall short of perfection and, following the Scriptures, he predicted a time of great wickedness in a world which had been made populous and prosperous as a result of its acceptance of the reign of Christ. Beyond the millennium then stood the last crisis and final revolution. Yet it is remarkable how his interest had shifted from the eternal kingdom into which souls enter one by one to the kingdom coming upon earth. He did not abandon the double doctrine of the future, but as he became more convinced of the power of God and of the reality of the Christian revolution the idea of the kingdom's coming to earth took a certain precedence. God had made possible what was impossible for men.

Many efforts have been made to account for the prevalence in American Christianity of the millenarian tendency. It has been erroneously ascribed to the early Calvinists and with greater reason to the left-wing Protestants. Yet the Awakening and the revivals seem above all to have made it the common and vital possession of American Christians. They brought the remote possibility very near. The rise in American faith of the idea of the coming kingdom was not due to an importation from the outside, that is, from rationalism or political idealism. It arose out of the Christian movement which had begun with the conviction of divine sovereignty, been led thence to the realization of Christ's kingdom and now saw clearly that the latter led toward the realization of man's everlasting hope.

Edwards was not the only one in whom this development came to light. Samuel Hopkins was another millenarian. Channing[8] says of him: "The millennium was his chosen ground. If any subject of thought possessed him above all others, I suppose it to have been this. The millennium was more than a belief to him. It has the freshness of visible things. He was at home in it. . . . Whilst to the multitude he seemed a hard, dry theologian, feeding on the thorns of controversy, he was living in a region of imagination, feeding on visions of a holiness and happiness which are to make earth all but heaven." His mil-

[8] William Ellery Channing, the great Unitarian of the early nineteenth century.

lenarianism like Edwards' was based upon faith in divine sovereignty and the experience of the order of grace. Neither of
these men thought of the coming kingdom in terms of supernatural appearances, save as the work of awakening, of regeneration and of the reconciliation of man to God could be
regarded as supernatural. They did not engage in the mathe-
matical calculations and astrological speculations of the literal-
ists. The millennium was the reign of Christ; the reign of Christ
was one of love to God, and therefore to man; and love came
through the "cleansing of the inward parts." "By the new
heaven and new earth is meant," Hopkins wrote, "the work of
redemption, or the church redeemed by Christ. . . . To suppose
that Christ shall come in his human nature to this earth, and
live here in his whole person visibly, a thousand years, before
the day of judgment," appears to be contrary to Scripture and
it is contrary to reason as well.

Though the instruments of the reign of Christ were spiritual
its sphere was this world. Edwards and Hopkins had no intention of saying to men that the fruits of the spirit were purely
spiritual, invisible to the eye. They insisted on the visibility of
Christ's rule in the social as well as in the personal sphere. The
time of the kingdom of heaven on earth, said Edwards, will be
"a time of great light and *knowledge*" especially in the doctrines
of religion; "it shall be a time of great *holiness;* . . . religion
shall in every respect be *uppermost* in the world." But it will
also be a time of "universal peace and a good understanding
among the nations of the world; . . . it will be a time of *excellent order* in the church of Christ," which is to be beautiful and
glorious, and it "will be a time of the greatest *temporal prosperity*" as well as of rejoicing. For "such a spiritual estate as
we have just described, has a natural tendency to health and
long life, . . . to procure ease, quietness, pleasantness, and
cheerfulness of mind, also wealth and a great increase of children," to which he adds that "temporal prosperity will also be
promoted by a remarkable blessing from heaven."

Hopkins prophesied that the millennium resulting from Christ's
coming in the hearts would be a time of eminent holiness or of
disinterested love to God and man. While he also emphasized

the increase of religious knowledge he added that men will have "sufficient leisure to pursue and acquire learning of every kind that will be beneficial to themselves and to society; . . . great advances will be made in all arts and sciences and in every useful branch of knowledge, which tends to promote the spiritual and eternal good of men, or their convenience and comfort in this life." It is, furthermore, to be a time of universal peace, love, and general and cordial friendship; religious unity will accompany political peace; it will be a "time of great enjoyment, happiness and universal joy" for spiritual but also for material reasons. Natural calamities will be prevented by divine providence; war with its impoverishment of men will have been abolished; intemperance and excess will be discarded; "the art of husbandry will be greatly advanced, and men will have skill to cultivate and manure the earth in a much better and easy way than ever before"; there will be "great improvement in the mechanic arts by which the earth will be subdued and cultivated, and all the necessary and convenient articles of life, such as utensils, clothing, buildings, etc. will be formed and made in a better manner, and with much less labor than they now are"; finally, "there will then be such benevolence and fervent charity . . . that all worldly things will be in a great degree and in the best manner common, so as not to be withheld from any who may want them."

Wesley, who although he was an Englishman was yet the most influential Methodist in America, offers us a further example of this millenarianism. He also foreshortened the future and brought the great revolution into the present, though it may be with more caution than the New Englanders displayed. He said:

"I cannot induce myself to think that God has wrought so glorious a work, to let it sink and die away in a few years: no, I trust, this is only the beginning of a far greater work; the 'dawn of the *latter day glory*.' . . . Before the end even the rich shall enter into the kingdom of God. Together with them will enter in the great, the noble, the honourable; yea, the rulers, the princes, the kings of the earth. Last of all, the wise, the learned, the men of genius, the philosophers, will be convinced that they are fools; will be 'converted and become as little children' and 'enter into the kingdom of God.' . . . All unprejudiced persons may see with their eyes, that [God] is already renewing the face of the earth and we have strong reason to hope that the work he has begun, he will carry on to the day of the Lord Jesus."

. . . The Quakers, as we have seen, had from the beginning anticipated the coming revolution and brought it into the present in the spiritual coming of Christ. Their millenarianism in the time of the Awakening and the revivals was somewhat less enthusiastic than that of Edwards and Hopkins. Perhaps their longer experience had taught them to be cautious. The revolution Woolman looked for was an individual event taking place in human souls. But the results which he expected were social—the freeing of slaves, the reduction of economic desire, the elimination of poverty through the decrease of wealth which requires poverty for its support, the cessation of war and the establishment of harmony among men.

Summarizing the development of the Evangelical expectation of the coming kingdom we may say that it was based solidly on the ideas of divine sovereignty and of the crisis in which this sovereignty involved sinful men; its second foundation was the idea of the kingdom of Christ, without which the coming kingdom was darkness and not light. The Awakening and the revivals tended to bring the coming kingdom into the present and to insist that the spiritual revolution could be and needed to be faced now. Then, as the success of this gospel became manifest, a great wave of expectancy came over men. The kingdom of God on earth had come very near, not as a result of moralistic endeavors after perfection but in consequence of the power of the gospel of reconciliation. It had come near through the miracle of mass conversion and through the validation of the promise that to those who sought first the kingdom and its righteousness all other things would be added. A Christian revolution was evidently taking place; a new day was dawning. In one sense of the word this gospel of the coming kingdom which had begun with men in their solitariness became definitely social, for it had social effects in mind. It insisted that the fruits of the personal revolution needed to appear and, insofar as the revolution was genuine, would appear in the whole common life, in science, art, agriculture, industry, church and state. There were variations among the leaders on many minor issues but on two major points they were in fundamental agreement. In the first place they knew that the promise could not be divorced from the crisis, or that there was no way into the kingdom of God on earth which did not pass through the darkness of loss and the death to the self. In the second place they agreed on the necessity of meeting the future crisis so far as possible in the present, of pressing into the kingdom which was coming inevitably with its judgment and its promise.

There was a third point of agreement, though the assent to it was one of common silence. The way into the coming kingdom lay, these men all believed, through the kingdom of Christ; the function of the church was to prepare men for crisis and for promise by proclaiming to them the gospel of repentance and faith rather than by persuading them to undertake specific political activity. It is a constant source of astonishment to many modern interpreters of the Evangelical movement that its leaders paid so little attention to politics. Edwards, as we have seen, was silent on the subject. Wesley and his followers were proud of the fact that politics were never mentioned in Methodist pulpits. Hopkins' mind was not on American independence, grateful as he was for it, but rather on the fact that the colonies could expect no deliverance out of their calamities or success of their warfare unless they repented of the sin of slavery and made all restitution in their power to its victims. Though Finney,[9] in the later time, was one of the chief inspirers of the antislavery movement he wrote his memoirs without referring to the Civil War. These astonishing silences were not due to indifference, as the last two examples show especially, but rather to the fact that such men regarded Revolution and Civil War as civil conflicts which would not settle the issue of the future. They did

---

[9] Charles Finney, a nineteenth-century revivalist, educator, and reformer.

not say, as their successors might, that such conflicts settle no question save the one of balance of power, but by their relative indifference toward them they showed that they had little faith in progress toward a true peace by any means save those of the Christian revolution. At the same time their confidence in the gospel was so great that they were not tempted to attach it to the chariots of secular parties. They represented again the spirit of those Old Testament loyalists of the kingdom who did not care greatly whether their nation remained politically independent or became powerful, but who wept over the unrighteousness of their people and died storming the ramparts of internal injustice.

19 FROM   *Alan Heimert*
Toward the Republic

Alan Heimert's Religion and the American Mind: From the Great Awakening to the Revolution *is the latest extensive study of the intellectual aspects of the Awakening. A professor of English at Harvard, he, like Niebuhr—with whom he has collaborated on another book— sees millenarian expectations in the Awakening, although Heimert stresses the peculiar association of America and the coming kingdom. He sees, too, a sense of American unity emanating from the intercolonial nature of the Awakening. Perhaps most important, however, is Heimert's reversal of Parrington's traditional equation. It was the enemies of the awakeners who, at least in their views of society, were anachronistic and the awakeners who were in the mainstream of the American mind.*

The Great Awakening was the series of religious revivals which, foreshadowed in the "refreshings" in New Jersey and

SOURCE. Alan Heimert, *Religion and the American Mind: From the Great Awakening to the Revolution,* Cambridge, Mass.: Harvard University Press, 1966, pp. 2–7, 9–10, 12, 13–20. Reprinted by permission of the publishers.

New England in 1734–1735, rose to intercolonial crescendo in
1740. In the estimation of the Awakening's most outspoken
critic, the revivals of the 1740's caused American Protestantism
to be "divided into Parties" for the first time since the Antinomian
Crisis of the 1630's. Actually, divisions existed within the American churches even before the Great Awakening. The Presbyterian Church, for instance, was torn by various issues throughout the 1730's. Likewise the Congregational ministers of New
England differed on such questions as the standards of church
memberships and, though no open breach had as yet appeared,
were aligning themselves into clearly identifiable groups. What
the Awakening did was crystallize these differences, giving them
objective form, and more importantly, expand them beyond the
clergy, making partisans of the laity as well. The "two armies,
separated, and drawn up in battle array" which Jonathan Edwards espied in 1742 were not clerical factions merely but hosts
whose confrontation embodied a fundamental cleavage within
the colonial populace itself.

One way of assessing the divisive consequences of the
Awakening is that which has often been followed by historians
of American Christianity—by considering the manner in which
the Awakening altered the denominational structure of the colonies. The two churches most directly involved in the revival
were fragmented. Presbyterianism was split into the Synod of
Philadelphia, dominated by the "Old Side" opposers of the
Awakening, and that of New York, whose members were the
"New Side" partisans of the revival. In Connecticut the Congregational Church was similarly, though not so dramatically,
sundered into "Old Lights" and "New Lights." There, also,
"Separate" conventicles were established in defiance of the parish
system and the semi-Presbyterial Saybrook Platform. Indeed,
throughout New England evangelical congregations declared
their independence from the associations and consociations that
had developed over the course of a century. Some defined
themselves as Baptists, and a few even as Presbyterians, but
most simply stood as autonomous, and disaffected, seceders from
the New England Way. Moreover, the revival impulse encouraged
the growth of Presbyterianism in the South, where previously

the Anglican Church had enjoyed a near monopoly. In Pennsylvania and New Jersey, and eventually in New England, the Baptists rose into new prominence as the beneficiaries of the revival. Throughout the North the Church of England, whose spokesmen were almost unanimously opposed to the Awakening, grew in numbers by virtue of its appeal to citizens offended by the enthusiasm of the revival.

But such a chronicle of sectarian division and proliferation obscures the fact that the "parties" thrown up by the Awakening were hardly so numerous as any listing of denominations might suggest. The fundamental post-Awakening division of the American mind was one that transcended both the inherited denominational structure and that created by the revival. There were in substance only *two* parties on the American religious scene in the period after the Great Awakening. Generally speaking, one consisted of the opponents of the revival, the other of its advocates, each of which over the succeeding years evolved a religious philosophy consistent with its involvement in and attitude toward the Awakening. These parties were of course not organizational entities, though it is true that the tendency of the century was toward more explicit and formal alignments. The parties into which American Protestantism was divided by the Awakening are best understood, and most accurately described, in intellectual terms. Both represented a casting off from the intellectual universe of Protestant scholasticism, and each marked the independent fulfillment of one of the strains that in Puritanism had been held in precarious balance: "piety" and "reason."

Such a division within Protestantism has long been acknowledged to be the intellectual characteristic of the eighteenth century. Indeed from one perspective what happened in America seems "merely one variant of a universal occurrence in Western culture." In England and on the Continent, as well as in the colonies, the "educated classes" turned to the "generalities of eighteenth-century rationalism," and the "spiritual hungers of the lower classes" found expression in revivals, in Pietism or what is called Evangelicalism. Such a division has been characterized by a recent chronicler of the Great Awakening in New England as the divergence and confrontation of the eighteenth-century forces of "Pietism" and the "Enlightenment."[10] However, the evangelical religion of the colonies differed markedly from the pietism of Europe, and the "rational religion" that arose to thwart the revival impulse was hardly identical to the faith of the Encyclopedists. The Great Awakening in America was a unique and profound crisis in the history of the "indigenous culture."

First of all, it perhaps needs to be stressed that the revival in America, unlike that promoted by the Wesleys in England, built and throve on the preaching of Calvinist doctrine. The "work of God is carried on here," George Whitefield wrote to John Wesley in early 1740, " (and that in a most glorious manner) by doctrines quite opposite to those you hold." The doctrines to which Whitefield referred were those of Wesley's sermon, *Free Grace,* in which the English evangelist had propounded what, in the parlance of the day, was deemed an "Arminian" theory of salvation. "Arminianism," a name derived from that of the Dutch theologian, Jacobus Arminius (1560–1609), had originally referred to the belief that grace is not irresistible, as Calvin had argued, but conditional. By the eighteenth century, however, the term was used less rigorously, often in conjunction with the names of such Trinitarian heresies as Pelagianism and Socinianism, to refer to any of a number of vague ideas expressive of impatience with the "rigid" and "harsh" doctrines of Calvinism. It was against such an "Arminianism," more appropriately called "rationalism," that the proponents of the American revival thought they were contending.

The Arminianism of the colonies had few affinities with the warmer faith of the Wesleys. Here it was the official theology only of the Church of England, which ascribed to man the power to work out his own salvation largely through the use of his rational powers. In the first quarter of the eighteenth century, moreover, not a few Congregational and Presbyterian preachers were also suggesting that man was not so depraved, nor God quite so sovereign, as orthodox doctrine had argued.

[10] Quoted from Perry Miller, "Jonathan Edwards and the Great Awakening" and Edwin S. Gaustad, *The Great Awakening in New England,* both cited elsewhere.

Such an undermining of Calvinism was in fact part of the inevitable working out of Puritanism's own modifications of strict
Calvinist doctrine. The "covenant theology" itself had made God
something less than an arbitrary and inscrutable being, and the
doctrine of "preparation" had come to imply, over the course of
the century, that man was capable of "willing" his own salvation.

The opening charge of the American revival was thus [a]
sermon of 1735 in which Edwards strove to restore the reformation doctrine of "justification by faith alone" as the "principal
hinge" of American Protestantism. In so challenging Arminianism, however, Edwards revealed that the two "schemes" which
he contrasted—the "evangelical" and the "legal"—were hardly
those traditionally identified with the terms Calvinist and
Arminian. For Edwards, in presenting evidence of "God's approbation of the doctrine of justification by faith alone," pointed,
not to the Pauline epistle, but to the numerous and "remarkable
conversions" experienced in Northampton in 1735. The focus
of debate was turning from the theoretic manner of God's operations to what He was actually accomplishing, and over the next
decade it moved even further away from the traditional issues
of the seventeenth century. During the Great Awakening the
contest of ideas was often phrased in the older terms. In 1740,
for instance, the young Presbyterian revivalist, Gilbert Tennent,
declared that "we may as easily reconcile Light and Darkness,
Fire and Water, Life and Death, as Justification partly by Works,
and partly by Grace." But even for Tennent, who yielded to
no man in the rigor of his Calvinism, the "principal hinge" of
the "evangelical scheme" was no longer a point of doctrine.
Though the issue was at first whether the Awakening was a
genuine "Work of God," the challenge of criticism and the response of evangelical spokesmen were such that the focus of
analysis quickly shifted from the will of God to the nature of
man. In this contest, the crux of Calvinism became the existen-
tial reality of the emotional conversion experience.

Similarly, the party that Edwards and Tennent opposed was
not perfectly characterized as an Arminian one. The advocates
of what Edwards styled the "legal scheme" eventually took to
themselves, by virtue presumably of their opposition to the "op-

pressive" doctrines of Calvinism, the name of "Liberals." But
their most distinguishing intellectual mark was the notion that
man is—or should be—a rational being, one who derives his
standards of virtuous behavior from an observation of the external world. A rationalist strain had of course been present in
American Puritanism from the beginning. One of the classic assumptions of the Puritan mind was that the will of God was to
be discerned in nature as well as in revelation. But in the late
seventeenth century, and with greater boldness by the 1720's,
voices had been heard in the colonies proclaiming that a knowledge of God's will was best derived, not from His word, but
from His works. The articulation of such a "religion of nature,"
attended as it was by the reversion of several of Connecticut's
more prominent young ministers to Episcopalianism, was one of
the developments that prompted the attack in the 1730's on
Arminianism. But with the Awakening the avowal of a rational
or "reasonable" theology was no longer limited to colonial
Anglicans. The notion that Christianity is pre-eminently a rational religion permeated the thinking of Old Side Presbyterianism, the Old Lights of Connecticut, and the Liberal clergy of
the neighborhood of Boston.

It was in Massachusetts that the creed of reason was most
conspicuously developed into a partisan ideology. There it
emerged, in the decades after the Awakening, as "the instrument of a group, or of an interest"—the group opposed to the
"enthusiasm" of the revival and the seeming unreason of evangelical religion. The premises of rational religion were first un-
folded in the criticisms of the Awakening published by the
leading Boston Liberal, Charles Chauncy. But the manifesto of
Congregational Liberalism was probably Ebenezer Gay's 1759
Harvard Dudleian Lecture, *Natural Religion*. Here Gay summarized the Liberal thesis that God has formed men as rational beings so they "might learn from his Works, what is good, and what
is required of them." The lessons of Scripture could only confirm what man was able to discover from the "Constitution of
Things, in their respective Natures and Relations." That Massachusetts Liberals were not alone in evolving such a theology
is indicated by the fact that the magnum opus of colonial ra-

tionalism was the *Elementa Philosophica* of the Anglican spokesman, Samuel Johnson of Connecticut. And this volume, in turn,
was recommended by Benjamin Franklin to all who would properly understand the true nature and bases of morality.

In sharp contrast to this studiously rationalistic religion of nature stood the "Calvinism" evolved in the decades after the
Awakening. Actually the Calvinists of eighteenth-century America were hardly subscribers to the theology of the *Institutes*. All
were familiar with, and frequently quoted, Edwards' classic dis-
claimer of "dependence on Calvin." If—as Samuel Hopkins
explained of Edwards—their "Principles were *Calvinistic*," they
"called no man, Father." They assumed the designation of Calvinist only, as one New Jersey Presbyterian announced, because
such terms were "exceeding useful" when one wished "to express
Complex Ideas." Yet the idea that essentially defined American
Calvinism was acknowledged to be a rather simple one—a belief in the "inward operation of the holy spirit in regeneration."
Herein they followed Jonathan Edwards in emphasizing the role
of the "affections" in religion and in making virtue dependent
on the reception of a "vital indwelling principle" from the Holy
Spirit.

In truth, the partisans of evangelical and emotional religion
were all in some degree under the intellectual dominion of Jonathan Edwards. Samuel Hopkins would undoubtedly have liked
to consider himself Edwards' only begotten intellectual offspring.
But he, like the Edwards of whom he wrote, "thought and
judged for himself, and was truly very much of an Original."
Just as close to Edwards in idea and spirit (and perhaps closer)
were the multitude of New Light and New Side preachers,
Separatists and Baptists, who, despite their minor differences
with Edwards, acknowledged him to be "the greatest pillar in
this part of ZION's BUILDING." Joseph Bellamy, Edwards' student
and friend, invariably cited his writings as the best books "on
experimental religion and vital piety since the days of inspiration." The Baptist Isaac Backus, though at one time in disagree-
ment with Edwards over the qualifications of the ministry, was
always ready to acknowledge him a writer of "pure truth" and
in later years, spoke of him as "our Edwards." Ebenezer Froth-

ingham, who was distraught when Edwards refused to accept the leadership of the Separates, continued to praise him as a defender of the revival and as a theologian and, after Edwards' death, saluted him as one who had "doubtless gone to heaven." Indeed a variety of ministers and men cherished the memory of the "late divine, whose praise is in all the churches," and for all of them Edwards' legacy consisted in the "many valuable volumes" which, as Gilbert Tennent consoled himself, this "ascending ELIJAH" had left as his mantle to American Calvinism. So well did they wear it, indeed, that the Calvinist ministry, averse as they were to invoking "great names" in support of ideas, were nevertheless more accurately "Edwardeans". . . .

For three and more decades the Calvinists (or Edwardeans) of America debated with the Liberals the questions of the nature of man and the character of God. In this confrontation the party lines of the revival were preserved essentially intact—and even reinforced. To be sure, not all the critics of the Awakening were full-blown rationalists. But as one defender of the revival observed, "the principal and most *inveterate Opposers*" were men of "Arminian and *Pelagian* Principles." The others, those whom he styled "only Deputy or second Hand Opposers," could not, however, long deny their fundamental differences with the Liberal opponents of the Awakening. Moreover, on the issues of the freedom of the human will, man's original sin, and, perhaps most importantly, the place of the emotions in religious experience, they came to acknowledge their affinities with the evangelical religion of the Awakening and of Edwards. . . .

There are many ways of looking at the division brought to America by the Awakening. One historian has concluded that the revival "cut a swath between rich and poor, stimulating the hostility that already divided them," and thus opened the way for "class conflict" in the colonies.[11] Clearly there were divisions and antagonisms among the American people in the period before the Awakening. One New England preacher, surveying the scene just before the impact of the revival had been felt,

[11] Quoting John C. Miller, "Religion, Finance, and Democracy in Massachusetts," cited above.

noted that New Englanders were distinguished by their "want of Brotherly Love (evident by their quarrelsome, litigious Disposition, and Law-Suits without number)." In many communities, disputes had arisen over the use and control of the common lands, and for years nearly every colony was racked by debates over the relative merits of specie and paper currency. The latter issue, revolving about the needs of the merchants for a "medium of trade" and the search by farmers for solutions to the problems of inflation, indebtedness, and the declining productivity of the land, had given rise to fairly hardheaded and pragmatic partisan contests. In each community and province hostility was expressed and exacerbated by such speculative programs as the "land-bank" scheme. All these controversies, in many of which the clergy participated, reflected the difficulty Americans were experiencing in coming to terms with their environment and with the involvement of the British government and economy in their affairs.

Far from stimulating these hostilities, however, the immediate effect of the religious revivals seems to have been a tempering of the fierce social, economic and political antagonisms that had racked the colonies since the beginning of the century. One glory of the Awakening in the eyes of those who approved it was the restoration of social and political concord to the villages and towns of the colonies. In 1741, Jonathan Edwards reported, the politicians and citizens of New England ceased their usual bickerings and contentions, and whole communities enjoyed a union and social harmony greater than that known "at any time during the preceding thirty years." . . . . The Calvinist ministry welcomed the Awakening, and long remembered it, as a golden age when men were not divided, personally or as partisans, over acquisition and distribution of the New World's resources.

Even in 1740, however, it escaped no one's notice that those who possessed "a greater measure of this world's goods" were less disposed toward the Awakening, or that evangelical religion held a greater appeal for the "lower classes" of American society. Yet at no time was the division between Calvinist and Liberal one merely of economic or social class—any more than the Great Awakening itself was "a revolt of the backcountry

producers from the stringent controls of the mercantile aristocracy."[12] Such interpretations of the eighteenth century do as
much violence to the American temper as accounts of the Great
Migration that portray New England as originally a plantation
of trade. The parties and debates of eighteenth-century American religion simply will not yield to the categories of Marx and
Beard, for the reason that the fundamental post-Awakening division was an intellectual one—one more aesthetic, in fact, than
economic or social. In the more accurate terms of H. Richard
Niebuhr, the division was between those who "saw the reality
of an order of being other than that walled and hemmed in
existence in which a stale institutional religion and bourgeois
rationalism were content to dwell" and those who did not.
What distinguished Americans, so far as the "great debate" of
the eighteenth century was concerned, was differences not of
income but, in substance, of taste.

Implicit in the "new light" of the revival was a foreswearing
of the pragmatic and rather hardheaded differences in policy
that before the Awakening had distinguished colonial partisanship. But from the moment when the eyes of some citizens of
the colonies were taken from their "ordinary secular business"
and turned to the "great things of religion," the stage was being
prepared for a new kind of party struggle, but one hardly less
vehement. In the contest between rational and evangelical religion was embodied, indeed, one of those fundamental value
disagreements which, according to many historians, America has
from the beginning been free. When Edwards first challenged
Arminian rationalism he proclaimed that the differences between
his "scheme" and the "legal one" were multiform and irrecon-
cilable. When the "foundation" is so different, he went on to
insist, "the whole scheme becomes exceeding diverse and contrary." Over the remainder of the century this contrariety was
to be manifested in nearly every area of thought and behavior. . . .

[12] Quoting Perry Miller, "Jonathan Edwards' Sociology of the Great Awakening," *New England Quarterly*, XXI (1948), and Richard D. Mosier, *The
American Temper* (Berkeley, 1952).

Almost any reading of the literature of pre-Revolutionary America soon yields the conclusion that many of the ideas apparently held in common by all American Protestants were not in fact shared. By virtue of the disparate intellectual universes out of which the utterances of Calvinism and Liberalism emerged, the same word as employed by each often contained and communicated a quite different meaning. . . . Two such words were among the most important in the vocabulary of eighteenth-century Americans: "liberty" and "union." Indeed, in the disparate connotations of these two words was encapsulated nearly the whole of the larger significance of the confrontation of rational and evangelical religion. The conflict between Liberalism and Calvinism was not, as is generally assumed, simply a token of the unwillingness of the latter to confess itself an anachronism in an age of reason and science. Rather the intellectual division and debate had implications for both the society of the colonies and its politics, and in such a context rational religion is not so readily identifiable as the more liberal of the two persuasions. Indeed the evidence attests that Liberalism was a profoundly elitist and conservative ideology, while evangelical religion embodied a radical and even democratic challenge to the standing order of colonial America.

From the very outset opponents of the revival sensed in the evangelical impulse a revolutionary potential. The "best of the people of all denominations," reported a Connecticut Anglican in 1742, feared that the "enthusiasts would shortly get the government into their hands and tyrannize over us." Ever afterward critics of evangelical thought were unable to debate with Calvinists (the latter complained) without having "something to say about the mad men of Munster, who they tell us rebelled against their civil rulers." Liberal fears seemed justified when, in the early 1760's, a New Light party took control of the Connecticut legislature. It seemed obvious that the "rigid enthusiasms and conceited notions" of the revival and evangelicalism were the sources of the "republican and mobbish principles and practices" of the insurgent party. The Calvinist ministry, "fond to a madness" of "popular forms of government," were, it was charged, responsible for Connecticut's "revolutionary" change of government. And when, a decade later, America was confronted by genuine revolution, it would often be concluded that what the colonies had awakened to in 1740 was none other than independence and rebellion. . . .

Some Thoughts Concerning the Present Revival of Religion, written and published by Jonathan Edwards in 1742, was in a profound sense the first national party platform in American history. Yet Edwards' thoughts seem totally divorced from all the topics of which partisan issues are presumably made. His thinking reveals the disengagement of the evangelical ministry and populace from the usual institutions and processes of government and politics. Edwards even dismisses as a relatively insignificant matter the outbreak of hostilities between Britain and Spain: "We in New England are now engaged in a more important war"—the battle between the opposition to the revival and those who wanted to encourage and forward it. Three years later the "serious people" of New England refused to enlist for the expedition against Louisburg until the magistrates somehow managed to persuade George Whitefield to bless the venture. Though Edwards eventually hailed the victory at Cape Breton as a Providential dispensation of momentous significance, the Calvinist mind continued to respond in the spirit of the *Thoughts on the Revival* to many of the great events of the next decades. In 1757, at the height of the French and Indian War, Samuel Davies was seeking an *"outpouring of the Spirit"* as the "grand, radical, all-comprehensive blessing" for Virginia. Even on the first day of January, 1775, Calvinist spokesmen were insisting that a revival of religion was the one thing needful, the "Sum of all Blessings," for the American colonies.

Nonetheless, it can be said that Edwards' judgment on the comparative importance of New England's two "wars" proved as prescient as his views on so many other subjects. For Edwards' *Thoughts,* like the Awakening he defended, was in a vital respect an American declaration of independence from Europe, and the revival impulse was one toward intercolonial union. To be sure, the Awakening was in inception a response to the changing conditions of American life as perceived on the level of the local community. But the Calvinist mind was such that Edwards' vision moved quickly outward from Northampton toward making all "New England a kind of heaven upon earth"—and from there to all America. Over the next decades evangelical thought so progressed that Davies sought the blessings of the spirit not for Hanover parish alone, but for his "country," and by 1775 Calvinists were looking for a gracious shower on what by then they saw as their "Nation and Land." The evangelical impulse, promoted almost entirely within the church and through "the ordinary means," was the avatar and instrument of a fervent American nationalism. . . .

Much of Calvinism's thrust, its radical and emphatic definitions of liberty and equality, emerged more as the premises and assumptions of doctrine than as an articulate program. Still, the Calvinist ministry aspired to understand the times in order that they, like the men of Issachar, might "know what Israel ought to do." In this respect, something of a watershed for the Calvinist mind was passed in 1755, when Aaron Burr, Edwards' son-in-law, published a sermon on imperial affairs which, omitting the doctrinal section, consisted entirely of commentary and advice on British and colonial government and policy. Over the next decades Calvinist spokesmen grew ever bolder in proposing programs for the accomplishment of what they took to be the general welfare. Many of their policies, indeed most of them, were directed toward the amelioration of domestic conditions—as, for instance, their demand for a "more effectual provision for the Instruction of our Children, in our Common Schools." In the Revolutionary period, domestic and imperial issues merged, and the evangelical scheme was translated into the political imperative that the colonial "poor" not be "squeezed, to support the corruption and luxury of the great."

As the last quotation suggests, the programmatic elements of Calvinism were invariably subordinated to, or conceived within, what the evangelical clergy considered the primary moral dimension of all activity, individual or communal. In the Revolutionary period, and before, the Calvinist mind responded to political challenge in terms of the felt obligation of both ministers and people to "fight sin always." Often the evangelical ministry concluded that "Sin" was the cause of all difficulties, "civil, ecclesiastical, and domestic," and they were ever ready to describe an opposing policy as a "mere ideal project, arising from the deceitfulness of sin." They also ranged rather widely in search of this "dreadful monster" and of means for overcoming and destroying sin. In sum, to the thought of post-Awakening and Revolutionary Calvinism can be traced that enduring quality of the American political mind that Richard Hofstadter has characterized as an impatience with "hard politics." In this sense the American tradition—of Populists and rank-and-file Jacksonians and Jeffersonians—was hardly the child of the Age of Reason. It was born of the "New Light" imparted to the American mind by the Awakening and the evangelical clergy of colonial America.

The contribution of eighteenth-century Calvinism to the making of the American public mind has been allowed to remain unappreciated. In fact it has been for the most part ignored, possibly because its thought evolved in a context of indifference to the stuff of which politics is made. Quite clearly Calvinists were not, in the quarter century or so after the Awakening, as disposed as the Liberal clergy to "pulpit politics." In 1750, for instance, Jonathan Mayhew, the young hope of Boston rationalism, proclaimed the clergy's right to engage in the avocation of *"preaching politics."* In the same year Edwards was reminding his Northampton congregation that the "mutual concerns of ministers and their people" were of infinitely greater moment "than any of the temporal concerns of men, whether private or public"—of more importance indeed than the fate of the greatest "earthly monarchs, and their kingdoms or empires." As late as the autumn of 1774 Calvinist ministers were insisting that they had a more important function than discussing "the civil rights of human nature" and just as sternly denying any but a recent interest in affairs of state.

Meanwhile the Liberal ministry were preaching intermittently on what they considered to be the rights of man. Indeed history has judged the rationalist clergy of eighteenth-century America to have been ideologically and even personally heralds of the Revolution. This notion, one of the more sophisticated myths concerning the American past, seems to be largely the creature of John Adams' memory, though Peter Oliver's registering of surprise and disgust at the spectacle of "respectable" ministers hawking "sedition" has helped to reinforce it. Nineteenth-century Unitarian historiography of course encouraged the thought that there is some inherent relationship between Liberal religion and the patriotism of the Revolution. Perhaps the ideas which informed the Declaration of Independence were in some way collaterally descended from those used to resist the revival and Calvinism, but the two were hardly blood relatives. Indeed, some twentieth-century historians have sensed a warmer faith at work in the "religious antecedents" of the Revolution. But they nevertheless concentrate almost exclusively on the words of the more familiar Chauncy and Mayhew. Thus is preserved the Liberal ministry's reputation as both the foremost among the Revolutionary clergy and the representatives of the mind of Protestant patriotism.

In the quarter century before 1776 the Liberal clergy did expound the ideas of the social contract and the law of nature—concepts derived from John Locke's *Second Treatise of Government*. A favored vehicle for exposition of these ideas was the New England Election Sermon. Delivered each spring in the capitals of Massachusetts and Connecticut, such sermons were intended as the ministry's edification of governor and legislature on the nature of civil government. On these occasions Liberal spokesmen articulated a nearly pure and simple Lockeanism. Passages and even whole sections of their sermons offer few hints of the speakers' clerical vocation. A paragraph like this one (from the Massachusetts Election Sermon of 1767) might as well have been composed by any American of the century who had read John Locke:

"Although there is a natural equality and independency among men yet they have voluntarily combined together, and by compact and mutual agreement, have entered into a social state, and bound themselves to the performance of a multitude of affairs, tending to the good; and to the avoiding of a multitude of injuries tending to the hurt and damage of the whole. And hence arises order and government, and a just regulation of all those matters which relate to the safety of the persons, lives, liberties, and property of individuals."

To extract such a passage from a clerical utterance, is, however, to distort and obscure the full meaning of the sermon and
even of the ideas of social contract and natural law as expounded
by the clergy. If the discourses of the ministry were assessed
only in terms of the extent to which each at some point repeated the postulates of John Locke, Liberals, and Calvinists—
with several signal exceptions—would appear nearly indistinguishable. Indeed one of the earliest uses of Locke's ideas was
in a pamphlet defending the revival and Separatism, which
opened with "a *short sketch* of what the celebrated Mr. Lock
in his *Treatise of Government* has largely demonstrated, and in
which it is justly to be presumed all are agreed who understand
the natural Right of Mankind." (This dissenter was also an
admirer of the celebrated Mr. Locke's *Letter on Toleration,*
which the Connecticut authorities, likewise exponents of the
idea of social contract, had forbidden to be printed or circulated
by a group of Yale undergraduates who wanted freedom for
evangelical religion.) Down through the years nearly every
Protestant minister in America, when commenting on civil
affairs, argued that though men give up "some part" of their
"natural liberty" on entering into society, no government could
violate their persons or property in an arbitrary manner. In
neither Liberal sermons nor Calvinist, however, did these echoes
and expositions of Lockean theory have the same meanings as
those attached to the concepts by the authors of the Declaration
of Independence.

Until and unless Liberals were confronted by imperial issues,
their interpretations of the social contract, particularly as they
applied to the internal affairs of the provinces, were careful and
methodical arguments for holding in check a populace that was
by no means conceived to be a community of natural equals.
Even in the Revolutionary period, when the Liberal spoke on
public affairs, his ideas were so phrased, and presented in such
a form, as to keep the "multitude" from involving itself in matters of state. Indeed the rationalist clergy were in the 1770's,
nearly to a man, if not outright Tories, then praying that the
magistrates and merchants to whose judgment they deferred
would find some compromise solution to the lamentable controversy between Britain and her colonies. They preached Locke

almost as a justification of the *status quo,* and even more importantly they did so by way of deploring and seeking to subdue the revolutionary enthusiasm that was, despite their hopes and efforts, arising in the American populace.

It was the more orthodox clergymen of America who infused the Lockean vocabulary with a moral significance, a severity and an urgency, and thereby translated the ideas of social contract and natural law into a spur to popular activity. In 1775, for instance, Moses Mather, latest of his illustrious name to occupy a pulpit, phrased *America's Appeal* largely in terms of Locke's defense of civil rights. But in so doing Mather eloquently affirmed the obligation of "all the members" of society to actively pursue and promote the general welfare. His appeal was not to the candid world but to the populace, who he believed already had a "right understanding" of the circumstances in which America found itself. His purpose was not to inform but to "render the exertions, the noble struggles of a brave, free and injured people, bold, rapid, and irresistible". . . . The multitudes of sermons delivered by more evangelical Calvinists were even more clearly devised as a means of stimulating the hearts and wills of the American people.

Herein consisted the most conspicuous difference between the utterances of Calvinists and of Liberals in the Revolutionary period. A further difference, and a not unrelated one, was that the evangelical ministry were not dependent on Locke for their political and social philosophy. Even when they employed his concepts of natural law and the social contract they were offering a counterstatement to the individualistic premises of Lockean theory. Eventually the spokesmen for the evangelical scheme produced a corpus of social and political thought that stands as the American counterpart of the writings of Rousseau. Radically communitarian in its assumptions and goals, such a theory sustained not only the Calvinist pressure toward independence and revolution but subsequent efforts to secure "the most equitable, rational, natural mode of civil government" for an independent America.

The Calvinist political philosophy, which centered finally not on the consent of the governed but on the general will of the community, was sustained by the equally fundamental evangelical conception that the purpose of public discourse was to activate men's wills as well as inform their minds. Whatever his particular thoughts, the Calvinist presented them in such a form and language that his political sermons were not vindications of action already taken but encouragement to further endeavor on the part of the populace. It is in this regard that our traditional view of the Revolution, its inspirations and its aspirations, may need some modification. As has been observed, a "pure rationalism" might have declared the independence of the American people, "but it could never have inspired them to fight for it."[13]

Quite apart from the question of the Revolution, the contrasts between Liberal and Calvinist social thought were possibly of less ultimate significance than the remarkable differences between their oratorical strategies and rhetorical practices. . . . It was the Calvinist conception of the pastor's role and his relationship to his people that led to the creation of an institutional framework within which men responded enthusiastically, in the 1770's, to the verbal promptings of their spiritual guides. Meanwhile, as the Calvinist clergy relied on the voluntary allegiance of their congregations and depended on what they came to call "the will of the people," the Liberals increasingly deferred to the civil authority. Within their own congregations they acquiesced in what was in effect an abandonment of the clergy's role as an intellectual force giving direction to the course of society.

The reconstitution of evangelical churches derived in part from explicit doctrine. Its profounder inspiration, however, seems to have been the radical imperative contained in Edwards' somewhat startling thesis of 1742—that God is, "as it were, under the power of his people." For at the heart of the evangelical scheme was an implicit democratization of the Deity—while Liberalism, for its part, devised a God who, however reasonable and forebearing, was nonetheless a sovereign from whom the prerogatives and privileges of the clergy de-

[13] Quoting Perry Miller, "From the Covenant to the Revival," in James W. Smith and A. Leland Jamison, eds., *The Shaping of American Religion,* I (Princeton, 1961) .

scended. Similarly, the intellectual premises of Calvinism were such that it reconceived and reconstituted the congregation as a vital communion of kindred spirits, its members animated by each other as well as by the minister. It was thus, often without seeming plan or direction, that Calvinism converted its ecclesiastical institutions into the bases of that "close union among themselves" to which its ultimate effectiveness "in Politicks" was attributed.

Indeed, in the evangelical churches of pre-Revolutionary America was forged that union of tribunes and people that was to characterize the early American Democracy. Yet it was not by ideas alone, nor even with social imagination, that the Calvinist ministry strove to energize the American populace. They differed from nearly all other eighteenth-century spokesmen in their recognition of the peculiar potency of the spoken word. . . .

Obviously the evangelical clergy were not alone among Americans in making the latter half of the eighteenth century something other than an age of reasoned discourse. The pamphleteers of the 1740's and 1750's, who charged that proposals for the immediate redemption of paper money betrayed the design and desire of certain "Lords of Mammon" to make "slaves and vassals of the commonality" were as emotional in their language as in their policies. So also were the numerous scriveners who in the early 1770's filled the colonial newspapers with allegations of perfidious British avarice. But their mode of discourse, if nothing else, clearly identified them with the eighteenth-century rational mind, which, to whatever degree enlightened, tended to agree with Benjamin Franklin that "Modern Political Oratory" was chiefly, and most properly, "performed by the Pen and Press." John Adams, for one, came to realize that the spoken word was also an essential instrument of persuasion (and so far as the Revolution was concerned, probably the more efficacious). But along with most of the more prominent lawyer-patriots of the day, he left that task to others and confined his public efforts to the medium of the written word.

The Liberal clergy too, despite their cultivation of a literary eloquence, were equally disposed to reach men primarily through the instrument of writing. It was in this regard that the evan-

gelical impulse, by its demurral from the standards of the eighteenth century, can be said to have inaugurated a new era in
the history of American public address. Though Puritanism had
of course always assumed the importance of "hearing the Word,"
an epoch can be dated from the arrival in the colonies of
George Whitefield and a realization of the remarkable effectiveness of his preaching. In 1741 Alexander Garden sought to
dismiss both Whitefield and the Awakening by bidding him
"only to put the *same* words, which from his mouth produced
the boasted effects, into the mouth of an *ordinary* speaker, and
see whether the same *effects* would be the consequence." Garden was paying unwitting and unwilling tribute to the skillful
manner of address of Whitefield, the "wonder of the world"
who, along with other evangelical preachers, launched an age
in which oratory would be recognized as the essential instrument
of moving the American public.

In emphasizing the Calvinists' mastery of the science and art
of the spoken word, it is not intended to deny the contribution
of the Liberal clergy to the Revolutionary impulse. It would
appear, however, that the utterances of Liberalism were hardly so
inflammatory as has been assumed, and that indeed its ideology
was more profoundly conservative than even the usual definition
of the Whig mind would allow. Similarly, the political thought
of Calvinism was such that in premises and implications it was
an evident anticipation of what, by the early nineteenth century,
emerged clearly as the more vital of American democratic traditions.

20 FROM *Perry Miller*
Crisis and Americanization

Powell M. Cabot Professor of American Literature at Harvard and the outstanding writer on the early American mind until his death in 1963, Perry Miller, through his disciples (including Alan Heimert) is still a major force among students of the American past. Thoughts and insights sparkle in profusion in his many works, including the two-volume The New England Mind *(New York, 1939 and Cambridge, 1953) and an intellectual biography,* Jonathan Edwards *(New York, 1949). Two points stand out in his brief article on "Jonathan Edwards and the Great Awakening." The first clears away a dispute about the relationship of the Awakening in America—a cataclysmic crisis in his view—to the concurrent religious emotionalism of western Europe by simply admitting the relationship and declaring it irrelevant to the effect on the American mind. The second makes what Parrington called "a little revolution"—the break-up of the traditional order during and after the Awakening—central to the process of Americanization.*

Although in the year 1740 some fairly flagrant scenes of emotional religion were being enacted in Boston, it was mainly in the Connecticut Valley that the frenzy raged and whence it spread like a pestilence to the civilized East. The Harvard faculty of that time would indeed have considered the Great Awakening a "crisis," because to them it threatened everything they meant by culture or religion or just common decency. It was a horrible business that should be suppressed and altogether forgotten. Certainly they would not have approved its being dignified as a starting-point in a series of great American crises.

As far as they could see, it was nothing but an orgy of the emotions. They called it—in the lexicon of the Harvard faculty

SOURCE. Perry Miller, "Jonathan Edwards and the Great Awakening," in Daniel Aaron, ed., *American Crisis: Fourteen Crucial Episodes in American History,* New York: Alfred A. Knopf, Inc., 1952, pp. 3–19. Reprinted by permission of the publisher.

this word conveyed the utmost contempt—"enthusiasm." It was
not a religious persuasion: it was an excitement of over-stimu-
lated passions that understandably slopped over into activities
other than the ecclesiastical and increased the number of bastards
in the Valley, where already there were too many. And above
all, in the Valley lived their archenemy, the deliberate instigator
of this crime, who not only fomented the frenzy but was so
lost to shame that he brazenly defended it as a positive advance
in American culture. To add insult to injury, he justified the
Awakening by employing a science and a psychological conception with which nothing they had learned at Harvard had
prepared them to cope.

It was certainly a weird performance. Edwards delivered his
revival sermons—for example the goriest, the one at Enfield
that goes by the title "Sinners in the Hands of an Angry God"
and is all that most people nowadays associate with his name—
to small audiences in country churches. In these rude structures
(few towns had yet prospered enough to afford the Georgian
churches of the later eighteenth century which are now the charm
of the landscape) the people yelled and shrieked, they rolled in
the aisles, they crowded up to the pulpit and begged him to
stop, they cried for mercy. One who heard him described his
method of preaching: he looked all the time at the bell rope
(hanging down from the roof at the other end of the church)
as though he would look it in two; he did not stoop to regard
the screaming mass, much less to console them.

Of course, in a short time the opinion of the Harvard faculty
appeared to be vindicated. In 1740 Edwards had writhing in the
churches not only his own people but every congregation he
spoke to, and he dominated the entire region. Ten years later
he was exiled, thrown out of his church and town after a vicious
squabble (the fight against him being instigated by certain of
the first citizens, some of them his cousins, who by adroit prop-
aganda mobilized "the people" against him), and no pulpit in
New England would invite this terrifying figure. He had no
choice but to escape to the frontier, as did so many misfits in
American history. He went to Stockbridge, where he eked out
his last years as a missionary to a lot of moth-eaten Indians.

Because of the works he produced under these—shall we call them untoward?—circumstances, and because he was still the acknowledged leader of the revival movement, he was invited in 1758 to become president of the College of New Jersey (the present-day Princeton), but he died a few weeks after his inauguration, so that his life really belongs to the Connecticut Valley.

One may well ask what makes such a chronicle of frenzy and defeat a crisis in American history. From the point of view of the social historian and still more from that of the sociologist it was a phenomenon of mass behavior, of which poor Mr. Edwards was the deluded victim. No sociologically trained historian will for a moment accept it on Edwards' terms—which were, simply, that it was an outpouring of the Spirit of God upon the land. And so why should we, today, mark it as a turning-point in our history, especially since thereafter religious revivals became a part of the American social pattern, while our intellectual life developed, on the whole, apart from these vulgar eruptions? The answer is that this first occurrence did actually involve all the interests of the community, and the definitions that arose out of it were profoundly decisive and meaningful. In that perspective Jonathan Edwards, being the most acute definer of the terms on which the revival was conducted and the issues on which it went astray, should be regarded—even by the social historian— as a formulator of propositions that the American society, having been shaken by this experience, was henceforth consciously to observe.

There is not space enough here to survey the Awakening through the vast reaches of the South and the Middle Colonies, nor even to list the intricate consequences for the social ordering of New England. The splintering of the churches and the increase of sectarianism suggest one way in which Americans "responded" to this crisis, and the impulse it gave to education, most notably in the founding of Princeton, is another. Such discussions, however valuable, are external and statistical. We come to a deeper understanding of what this crisis meant by examining more closely a revelation or two from the most self-conscious— not to say the most literate—theorist of the Awakening.

The theme I would here isolate is one with which Edwards dealt only by indirection. He was skilled in the art of presenting ideas not so much by expounding as by vivifying them, and he achieved his ends not only by explicit statement but more often by a subtle shift in emphasis. In this case, it is entirely a matter of divining nuances. Nevertheless, the issue was present throughout the Awakening and, after the temporary manifestations had abated, on this proposition a revolution was found to have been wrought that is one of the enduring responses of the American mind to crisis.

I mean specifically what it did to the conception of the relation of the ruler—political or ecclesiastical—to the body politic. However, before we can pin down this somewhat illusive development, we are confronted with the problem of whether the Great Awakening is properly to be viewed as a peculiarly American phenomenon at all. It would be possible to write about it— as has been done—as merely one variant of a universal occurrence in Western culture. Between about 1730 and 1760 practically all of Western Europe was swept by some kind of religious emotionalism. It was present in Germany, Holland, Switzerland, and France, and in Catholic circles there was an analogous movement that can be interpreted as an outcropping of the same thing, and that the textbooks call "Quietism." And most dramatically, it was present in England with the Wesleys, Whitefield, and Methodism.

Once this international viewpoint is assumed, the American outburst becomes merely one among many—a colonial one at that—and one hesitates to speak about it as a crisis in a history specifically American. What was at work throughout the Western world is fairly obvious: the upper or the educated classes were tired of the religious squabbling of the seventeenth century, and turned to the more pleasing and not at all contentious generalities of eighteenth-century rationalism; the spiritual hungers of the lower classes or of what, for shorthand purposes, we may call "ordinary" folk were not satisfied by Newtonian demonstrations that design in the universe proved the existence of God. Their aspirations finally found vent in the revivals, and in each country we may date the end of a Calvinist or scholastic or, in short, a theological era by the appearance of these movements, and thereupon mark what is by now called the era of Pietism or Evangelicalism.

In this frame of reference, the Great Awakening was only incidentally American. It is only necessary to translate the European language into the local terminology to have an adequate account. In this phraseology, the Great Awakening in New England was an uprising of the common people who declared that what Harvard and Yale graduates were teaching was too academic. This sort of rebellion has subsequently proved so continuous that one can hardly speak of it as a crisis. It is rather a chronic state of affairs. And in this view of it, the uprising of 1740 belongs to the history of the eighteenth century rather than to any account of forces at work only on this continent.

Told in this way, the story will be perfectly true. Because we talk so much today of the unity of Western European culture, maybe we ought to tell it in these terms, and then stop. But on the other hand there is a curiously double aspect to the business. If we forget about Germany and Holland and even England—if we examine in detail the local history of Virginia, Pennsylvania, and New England—we will find that a coherent narrative can be constructed out of the cultural developments in each particular area. The Awakening can be seen as the culmination of factors long at work in each society, and as constituting, in that sense, a veritable crisis in the indigenous civilization.

II

The church polity established in New England was what today we call Congregational. This meant, to put it crudely, that a church was conceived as being composed of people who could certify before other people that they had a religious experience, that they were qualified to become what the founders called "visible saints." The founders were never so foolish as to suppose that everybody who pretended to be a saint *was* a saint, but they believed that a rough approximation of the membership to the Covenant of Grace could be worked out. A church was composed of the congregation, but these were only the professing Christians. The rest of the community were to be rigorously excluded; the civil magistrate would, of course, compel them to come to the church and listen to the sermon, collect from them a tax to support the preacher, but they could not be actual members. Those who qualified were supposed to have had something happen to them that made them capable—as the reprobate was not—of swearing to the covenant of the church. They were able, as the others were not, *physically* to perform the act.

The basic contention of the founders was that a church is based upon the covenant. Isolated individuals might be Christians in their heart of hearts, but a corporate body could not come into being unless there was this preliminary clasping of hands, this taking of the official oath in the open and before all the community, saying, in effect: "We abide by this faith, by this covenant." In scholastic language, the congregation were the "matter" but the covenant was the "form" of the church. They objected above all things to the practice in England whereby churches were made by geography; that a lot of people, merely because they resided in Little Willingdon, should make the church of Little Willingdon, seemed to them blasphemy. That principle was mechanical and unreal; there was no spiritual participation in it—no covenant.

That was why they (or at any rate the leaders and the theorists) came to New England. On the voyage over, in 1630, John Winthrop said to them: "For wee must Consider that wee shall be as a Citty vppon a Hill, the eies of all people are vppon us." They had been attempting in England to lead a revolution; after the king's dismissal of Parliament in 1629 it looked as though there was no longer any hope of revolution there, and so they migrated to New England, to build the revolutionary city, where they could exhibit to Englishmen an England that would be as all England should be.

The essence of their conception was the covenant. As soon as they were disembarked, as soon as they could collect in one spot enough people to examine each other and acknowledge that each seemed visibly capable of taking the oath, they incorporated churches—in Boston, Charlestown, and Watertown, and, even in the first decade, in the Connecticut Valley. But we must always remember that even in those first days, when conviction was at its height, and among so highly selected and dedicated numbers as made up the Great Migration, only about one fifth of the population were found able, or could find themselves able, to take the covenant. The rest of them—with astonishingly few exceptions—were not "enabled" and praying for the grace that might yet empower them.

From that point on, the story may seem somewhat peculiar, but after a little scrutiny it becomes an old and a familiar one: it is what happens to a successful revolution. The New Englanders did not have to fight on the barricades or at Marston Moor; by the act of migrating, they *had* their revolution. Obeying the Biblical command to increase and multiply, they had children—hordes of them. Despite the high rate of infant mortality, these children grew up in New England knowing nothing, except by hearsay and rumor, of the struggles in Europe, never having lived amid the tensions of England. This second generation were, for the most part, good people; but they simply did not have—they could not have—the kind of emotional experience that made them ready to stand up before the whole community and say: "On Friday the 19th, I was smitten while plowing Deacon Jones's meadow; I fell to the earth, and I knew that the grace of God was upon me." They were honest people, and they found it difficult to romanticize about themselves— even when they desperately wanted to.

In 1662 the churches of New England convoked a synod and announced that the children of the primitive church members were included in the covenant by the promise of God to Abraham. This solution was called at the time the Halfway Covenant, and the very phrase itself is an instructive demonstration of the New Englanders' awareness that their revolution was no longer revolutionary. These children, they decided, must be treated as members of the church, although they had not had the kind of experience that qualified their fathers. They must be subject to discipline and censures, because the body of the saints must be preserved. But just in case the authorities might be mistaken, they compromised by giving to these children only a "halfway" status, which made them members but did not admit them to the Lord's Supper.

This provision can easily be described as a pathetic, where it is not a ridiculous, device. It becomes more comprehensible when we realize that it was an accommodation to the successful revolution. Second and third generations grow up inheritors of a revolution, but are not themselves revolutionaries.

For the moment, in the 1660's and 1670's, the compromise worked, but the situation got worse. For one thing, New England suffered in King Philip's War, when the male population was decimated. Then, in 1684, the charter of Massachusetts was revoked, and after 1691 the colony had to adjust itself to the notion that its governor was imposed by the royal whim, not by the election of the saints. Furthermore, after 1715 all the colonies were prospering economically; inevitably they became more and more concerned with earthly things—rum, land, furs. On the whole they remained a pious people. Could one go back to Boston of 1710 or 1720—when the ministers were asserting that it was as profligate as Babylon—I am sure that one would find it, compared with modern Hollywood, a strict and moral community. Nevertheless, everybody was convinced that the cause of religion had declined. Something had to be done.

As early as the 1670's the ministers had found something they could do: they could work upon the halfway members. They could say to these hesitants: "You were baptized in this church, and if you will now come before the body and 'own' the covenant, then your children can in turn be baptized." Gradually a whole segment of doctrine was formulated that was not in the original theory—which made it possible to address these citizens who were neither outside the pale nor yet snugly inside, which told them that however dubious they might be as saints, visible or invisible, they yet had sufficient will power to perform the public act of "owning the covenant."

With the increasing pressures of the late seventeenth and early eighteenth centuries, the practice of owning the covenant gradually became a communal rite. It was not enough that the minister labored separately with John or Elizabeth to make an acknowledgement the next Sunday: a day was appointed when all the Johns and Elizabeths would come to church and do it in unison, the whole town looking on. It is not difficult to trace through the increasing re-enactments of this ceremony a mounting crescendo of communal action that was, to say the least, wholly foreign to the original Puritanism. The theology of the founders conceived of man as single and alone, apart in a corner or in any empty field, wrestling with his sins; only after he had survived this experience in solitude could he walk into the church and by telling about it prove his right to the covenant. But this communal confession—with everybody doing it together, under the urgencies of an organized moment—this was something new, emerging so imperceptibly that nobody recognized it as an innovation (or rather I should say that some did, but they were shouted down) that by the turn of the century was rapidly becoming the focus for the ordering of the spiritual life of the town.

The grandfather of Jonathan Edwards, Solomon Stoddard of Northampton, was the first man who openly extended the practice of renewal of covenant to those who had never been in it at all. In short, when these occasions arose, or when he could precipitate them, he simply took into the church and up to the Lord's Supper everyone who would or could come. He called the periods when the community responded *en masse* his "harvests," of which he had five: 1679, 1683, 1696, 1712, 1718. The Mathers attacked him for so completely letting down the bars, but in the Connecticut Valley his success was envied and imitated.

The Great Awakening of 1740, seen in the light of this development, was nothing more than the culmination of the process. It was the point at which the method of owning the covenant became most widely and exultingly extended, in which the momentum of the appeal got out of hand, and the ministers, led by Jonathan Edwards, were forced by the logic of evolution not only to admit all those who would come, but to excite and to drive as many as possible, by such rhetorical stimulations as "Sinners in the Hands of an Angry God," into demanding entrance.

All of this, traced historically, seems natural enough. What 1740 did was present a number of leading citizens, like the Harvard faculty, with the results of a process that had been going on for decades but of which they were utterly ignorant until the explosion. Then they found themselves trying to control it or censure it by standards that had in fact been out of date for a century, although they had all that while professed them in filial piety. In this sense—which I regret to state has generally eluded the social historian—the Great Awakening was a crisis in the New England society.

Professional patriots, especially those of New England descent, are fond of celebrating the Puritans as the founders of the American tradition of rugged individualism, freedom of conscience, popular education, and democracy. The Puritans were not rugged individualists; they did indeed believe in education of a sort, but not in the "progressive" sense; they abhorred freedom of conscience; and they did not believe at all in democracy. They advertised again and again that their church polity was not democratic. The fact that a church was founded on a covenant and that the minister happened to be elected by the mass of the church—this emphatically did not constitute a democracy. John Cotton made the position of the founders crystal clear when he told Lord Say and Seal that God never ordained democracy as a fit government for either church or commonwealth; although at first sight one might suppose that a congregational church was one, in that the people chose their governors, the truth was that "the government is not a democracy, if it be administered, not by the people, but by the governors." He meant, in short, that even though the people did select the person, the office was prescribed; they did not define its functions, nor was it responsible to the will or the whim of the electors. "In which respect it is, that church government is iustly denied . . . to be democratical, though the people choose their owne officers and rulers."

The conception ran through every department of the social thinking of New England in the seventeenth century, and persisted in the eighteenth up to the very outbreak of the Awakening. The essence of it always was that though officers may come into their office by the choice of the people, or a number of people, nevertheless the definition of the function, dignity, and prerogatives of the position does not depend upon the intentions or wishes of the electorate, but upon an abstract, divinely given, absolute prescription, which has nothing—in theory—to do with such practical or utilitarian considerations as may, at the moment of the election, be at work among the people.

The divine and immutable pattern of church government was set, once and for all, in the New Testament; likewise, the principles of political justice were given in an eternal and definitive form. The machinery by which a particular man was chosen to fulfill these directives (as the minister was elected by the vote of a congregation, or as John Winthrop was made governor of the Massachusetts Bay Company by a vote of the stockholders) was irrelevant. The existence of such machinery did not mean that the elected officer was in any sense responsible to the electorate. He knew what was expected of him from an entirely other source than their temporary passions; he knew what he, upon becoming such a being, should do—as such!

The classic statement, as is widely known, was the speech that John Winthrop delivered before the General Court on July 3, 1645. He had been accused by the democracy of overstepping the limits of his power as a magistrate, and was actually impeached on the accusation. He was acquitted, and thereupon made this truly great declaration. He informed the people that the liberty of the subject may sometimes include, as happily it did in Massachusetts, the privilege of selecting this or that person for office, but that it did not therefore mean the right to tell the officer what he should do once he was installed. The liberty that men enjoy in civil society, he said, "is the proper end and object of authority, and cannot subsist without it." It is not a liberty to do what you will, or to require the authority to do what you want: "It is a liberty to do that only which is good, just, and honest." Who defines the good, the just, and the honest? Obviously, the authority does.

In other words, the theory of early New England was basically medieval. Behind it lay the conception of an authoritative scheme of things, in which basic principles are set down once and for all, entirely before, and utterly without regard for, political experience. The formulation of social wisdom had nothing to do with the specific problems of any one society. It was not

devised by a committee on ways and means. Policy was not to
be arrived at by a discussion of strategy—for example (in modern terms), shouldn't we use the atomic bomb now? This sort
of argument was unavailing, because the function of government
was to maintain by authority that which was inherently—and
definably—the true, just, and honest.

In Hartford, Connecticut, a colleague of the great Thomas
Hooker, the most comprehensive theorist of the Congregational
system, summarized the argument by declaring that Congregationalism meant a silent democracy in the face of a speaking
aristocracy. There might be something which we call democracy
in the form of the church, but the congregation had to keep
silent when the minister spoke. And yet, for a hundred years
after the death of Hooker, this strange process went on inside
the institution. The official theory remained, down to the time
of Edwards, that the spokesman for the society—be he governor
or minister—told the society, by right divine, what it should or
should not do, without any regard to its immediate interests,
whether emotional or economic. He had laid upon him, in fact,
the duty of forgetting such wisdom as he might have accumu-
lated by living as a particular person in that very community or
having shared the hopes and qualities of precisely these people.

What actually came about, through the device of renewing the
covenant, was something that in fact completely contradicted the
theory. (We must remember that the church was, during this
century, not merely something "spiritual," but the institutional
center of the organized life.) Instead of the minister standing
in his pulpit, saying: "I speak; you keep quiet," he found himself, bit by bit, assuming the posture of pleading with the people:
"Come, and speak up." He did not know what was happening.
He began to find out only in the Great Awakening, when the
people at last and multitudinously spoke up.

III

The greatness of Jonathan Edwards is that he understood
what had happened. But note this carefully. He was not Thomas

Jefferson; he did not preach democracy, and he had no interest whatsoever in any social revolution. He was the child of this aristocratic, medieval system; he was born to the purple, to ecclesiastical authority. But he was the man who hammered it home to the people that they *had* to speak up, or else they were lost.

Edwards was a Puritan and a Calvinist. He believed in predestination and original sin and all those dogmas which college students hold to be outworn stuff until they get excited about them as slightly disguised by Franz Kafka. Edwards did not submit these doctrines to majority vote, and he did not put his theology to the test of utility. But none of this was, in his existing situation, an issue. Granting all that, the question he had to decide was: What does a man do who leads the people? Does he, in 1740, say with the Winthrop of 1645 that they submit to what he as an ontologist tells them is good, just, and honest?

What he realized (lesser leaders of the Awakening, like Gilbert Tennent, also grasped the point, but none with the fine precision of Edwards) was that a leader could no longer stand before the people giving them mathematically or logically impregnable postulates of the eternally good, just, and honest. That might work in 1640, or in Europe (where to an astonishing extent it still works), but it would not work in Northampton. By 1740 the leader had to get down amongst them, and bring them by actual participation into an experience that was no longer private and privileged, but social and communal.

In other words, he carried to its ultimate implication—this constitutes his "relation to his times," which no purely social historian can begin to diagnose—that slowly forming tendency which had been steadily pressing through enlargements of the ceremonial owning of the covenant. He carried it so far that at last everybody could see what it really did mean. Then the Harvard faculty lifted its hands in horror—because this ritual, which they had thought was a segment of the cosmology of John Winthrop, was proved by Edwards's use to flow from entirely alien principles. For this reason, his own Yale disowned him.

IV

In the year 1748 Edwards's revolutionary effort—his leadership of the Awakening must be seen as resumption of the revolutionary thrust that had been allowed to dwindle in the Halfway
Covenant—was almost at an end. The opposition was mobiliz-
ing, and he knew, even before they did, that they would force
him out. When the fight had only begun, his patron and friend,
his one bulwark in the civil society, Colonel John Stoddard,
chief of the militia and warden of the marches, died. There
was now no civil power that could protect him against the hatred
of the "river gods." Out of all New England, Stoddard had been
really *the* outstanding magistrate in that tradition of aristocratic
leadership which had begun with Winthrop and had been sustained through a massive succession. As was the custom in New
England, the minister gave a funeral sermon; Edwards preached
over the corpse of the town's greatest citizen—who happened,
in this case, to be also his uncle and his protector. Those who
were now certain, with Colonal Stoddard in the ground, that
they could get Edwards's scalp were in the audience.

Edwards delivered a discourse that at first sight seems merely
one more Puritan eulogy. He told the people that when great
and good men like Stoddard are taken away, this is a frown of
God's displeasure, which indicates that they ought to reform their
vices. This much was sheer convention. But before he came, at
the end, to the traditional berating of the populace, Edwards
devoted the major part of his oration to an analysis of the
function and meaning of authority.

It should be remembered that Winthrop had commenced the
New England tradition by telling the people that they had the
liberty to do only that which is in itself good, just, and honest;
that their liberty was the proper end and object of authority
thus defined; that the approbation of the people is no more than
the machinery by which God calls certain people to the exercise
of the designated powers. And it should also be borne in mind
that these powers are given apart from any consideration of
the social welfare, that they derive from ethical, theological—*a
priori*—considerations.

Jonathan Edwards says that the supreme qualification of a
ruler is that he be a man of "great ability for the management of
public affairs." This is his first and basic definition! Let us
follow his very words, underlining those which carry revolutionary significance. Rulers are men "of great *natural* abilities" who
are versed in discerning "those things wherein the *public welfare
or calamity consists,* and the proper *means* to avoid the one and
promote the other." They must have lived among men long
enough to learn how the mass of them disguise their motives, to
"unravel the false, subtle arguments and cunning sophistry that
is often made use of to defend *iniquity."* They must be men
who have improved their talents by—here are his great criteria—*study, learning, observation,* and *experience.* By these
means they must have acquired "skill" in public affairs, "a great
understanding of *men and things,* a great *knowledge of human
nature,* and of the way of *accommodating* themselves to it."
Men are qualified to be rulers if and when they have this "very
extensive knowledge of men with whom they are concerned,"
and when also they have a full and particular understanding
"of the *state and circumstances* of the country or people that
they have the care of." These are the things—not scholastical
articles—that make those in authority "fit" to be rulers!

Look closely at those words and phrases: skill, observation,
men and things, state and circumstances—above all, experience!
Is this the great Puritan revivalist? It is. And what is he saying,
out of the revival? He is telling what in political terms the
revival really meant: that the leader has the job of accommodating himself to the realities of human and, in any particular
situation, of social, experience. No matter what he may have
as an assured creed, as a dogma—no matter what he may be
able to pronounce, in the terms of abstract theology, concerning predestination and original sin—as a public leader he must
adapt himself to public welfare and calamity. He cannot trust
himself to *a priori* rules of an eternal and uncircumstanced good,
just, and honest. There are requirements imposed by the office;
authority does indeed consist of propositions that pertain to it,
but what are they? They are the need for knowing the people,
the knack of properly manipulating and operating them, the wit

to estimate their welfare, and the cunning to foresee what may become their calamity.

When we are dealing with so highly conscious an artist as Edwards, we not only are justified in submitting so crucial a paragraph to close analysis, we are criminally obtuse if we do not. Most of my effort in my recent studies of him comes down to persuading people to read him. So it becomes significant to note what Edwards does immediately after his radically new definition of the ruler. Following his own logic, he is prepared at once to attack what, in the state and circumstances of the Connecticut Valley, constituted the primary iniquity, from which the greatest social calamity might be expected.

He does it without, as we might say, pulling punches: a ruler must, on these considerations of welfare, be unalterably opposed to all persons of "a mean spirit," to those "of a narrow, private spirit that may be found in little tricks and intrigues to promote their private interest, [who] will shamefully defile their hands to gain a few pounds, are not ashamed to hip and bite others, grind the faces of the poor, and screw upon their neighbors; and will take advantage of their authority or commission to line their own pockets with what is fraudulently taken or withheld from others." At the time he spoke, there sat before him the merchants, the sharp traders, the land speculators of Northampton; with the prompt publication of the sermon, his words reached similar gentlemen in the neighboring towns. Within two years, they hounded him out of his pulpit.

The more one studies Edwards, the more one finds that much of his preaching is his condemnation, in this language of welfare and calamity rather than of "morality," of the rising and now rampant businessmen of the Valley. It was Edward's great perception—and possibly his greatest value for us today is precisely here—that the get-rich-quick schemes of his contemporaries were wrong not from the point of view of the eternal values but from that of the public welfare. The ruler, he said, must know the "theory" of government in such a way that it becomes "natural" to him, and he must apply the knowledge he has obtained by study and observation "to that business, so as to perform it most advantageously and effectually." Here he was, at the moment his protector was gone, and he knew that he was lost, telling those about to destroy him that the great man is he who leads the people by skill and experiential wisdom and not by making money.

It is further revealing that, after Edwards had portrayed the ruler in this frame of utility and calculation, when he came to his fourth point he then for the first time said that the authority ought to be a pious man, and only in his fifth and last did he suggest the desirability of a good family. For Winthrop these qualifications had been essentials of the office; for Edwards they were radically submitted to a criterion of utility. "It also contributes to the strength of a man in authority . . . when he is in such circumstances as give him advantage for the exercise of his strength, for the public good; as his being a person of honorable descent, of a distinguished education, his being a man of estate." But note—these are all "useful" because they "add to his strength, and increase his ability and advantage to serve his generation." They serve "in some respect" to make him more effective. It had never occurred to John Winthrop that the silent democracy should imagine for a moment that the elected ruler, in church or state, should be anyone but a pious, educated, honourably descended person, of adequate economic substance. Edwards (who was pious, educated, and very well descended, but not wealthy) says that in some respect these advantages are helps to efficiency.

From one point of view, then, this was what actually was at work inside the hysterical agonies of the Great Awakening. This is one thing they meant: the end of the reign over the New England and American mind of a European and scholastical conception of an authority put over men for the good of men who were incapable of recognizing their own welfare. This insight may assist us somewhat in comprehending why the pundits of Boston and Cambridge, all of whom were rational and tolerant and decent, shuddered with a horror that was deeper than mere dislike of the antics of the yokels. To some extent, they sensed that the religious screaming had implications in the realm of society, and those implications they—being businessmen and speculators, as were the plutocracy of Northampton—did not like.

Again, I would not claim too much for Edwards, and I have no design of inscribing him among the prophets of democracy or the New Deal. What he marks—and what he alone could make clear—is the crisis from which all the others (or most of them) dealt with in this book depend, that in which the social problem was taken out of the arcana of abstract morality and put into the area of skill, observation, and accommodation. In this episode, the Americans were indeed participating in an international movement; even so, they came—or Edwards brought them—to sharper formulations of American experience. What the Awakening really meant for Americans was not that they too were behaving like Dutchmen or Germans or Lancashire workmen, but that in the ecstasy of the revival they were discovering, especially on the frontier, where life was the toughest, that they rejected imported European philosophies of society. They were now of themselves prepared to contend that the guiding rule of this society will be its welfare, and the most valuable knowledge will be that which can say what threatens calamity for the state.

21 FROM   *Richard L. Bushman*
A Psychological Earthquake

Perry Miller viewed the breakup of the traditional order from the standpoint of Jonathan Edwards. Richard L. Bushman views it from the standpoint of society as a whole in his analysis of "character and the social order in Connecticut" in the eighteenth century. Resorting to a simplistic behavioralism—the basic notion of which is that actions are determined by the value of resulting pain (negative) or pleasure

SOURCE. Richard L. Bushman, *From Puritan to Yankee: Character & the Social Order in Connecticut, 1690–1765,* Cambridge, Mass.: Harvard University Press, pp. 187–195. Copyright, 1967, by the President and Fellows of Harvard College. Reprinted by permission of the publishers.

(positive)—he juxtaposes three values to produce a tension relieved only by the conversion experience of the Awakening: subservience to authority and the social order (negative) reinforced by God's will (positive), the sum in opposition to individual prosperity, well-being and advancement (positive). By the end of the Awakening the three values stood in different order. As he writes, "a psychological earthquake had reshaped the human landscape."

What had happened to prepare so large a portion of the population for this momentous change? What power was there in the words of a sermon to plunge a person into the blackest despair and then bring him out into light and joy, a new man? The answer lay in the revivalist's message. He told his listeners that they were enemies of God and certain to be damned. When sufficiently crushed by their sinfulness, they learned that good works would never save them but that God's free grace would. This idea lifted men from their misery and restored them to confidence in God's love. Men who had come to believe that they were damnably guilty were ready to rely on unconditional grace.

The peculiarities of the Puritan personality partly account for the listeners' conviction that they were worthy only of damnation and hence wholly dependent on God's favor. Hypersensitive to overbearing authority, and always afraid of its destructive power, Puritans instinctively resisted whenever it threatened— but not without guilt. Since they could not avoid conflicts, surrounded as they were by rulers and laws, they lived in the consciousness of multiple offenses. They did not separate earthly clashes with authority from sins against God, for they believed the rulers and laws derived their power from the heavens. With life so structured, deep feelings of guilt inevitably grew.

These tensions had existed long before 1740, but despite pleas from the clergy, conversions had been few. Not until 1721 were any appreciable number of men sufficiently overpowered by their own sinfulness to rely wholly on God's grace and be converted. Two conditions prepared men for conversion: an increased desire for material wealth that ministers called worldly pride or covetousness, and the growing frequency of clashes with authority entailed in the pursuit of wealth. Both were the results of economic expansion, and both were, in the Puritan mind, offenses against God.

The Puritans' feelings about wealth were ambigious. Even the most pious associated it with a secure place in the community and divine approval, and everyone accorded great respect to rich men, numbering them among the rulers of society. Prosperity was a sign of good character: all were expected to practice industry and thrift, the virtues that brought the rewards of wealth. To some extent worldly success was a token of God's favor: none felt constrained to stint their efforts to prosper in their callings.

Yet the dangers of riches also were well known. The rich were prone to *"fall into Temptation,"* Cotton Mather warned, and be *"drowned in Perdition."* "There is a venom in *Riches,"* he said, "disposing our depraved Hearts, to cast off their *Dependence* on *God."* It was a maxim of the Jeremiads that "where a Selfish, Covetous spirit and Love of this world prevails, there the Love of God decayeth." When Connecticut's first published poet, Roger Wolcott, occupied himself with the theme of the divine wrath visited on seekers of earthly honor and wealth, he explained that he might have chosen the path of pride himself, "but that I see Hells flashes folding through Eternities." In this world money answered everything but a guilty conscience.

The contradiction in the prevailing attitudes toward wealth perplexed both the ministers and the people. Pastors complained that men excused avarice as justifiable enterprise. "They will plead in defense of a Worldly Covetous spirit, under the colour or specious pretence of Prudence, Diligence, Frugality, Necessity." Cotton Mather lamented that even the farmer was grasped with worldliness, yet he turned away rebukes with the assertion that he was merely pursuing his calling as a husbandman. The people could not distinguish respectable industry from covetousness: their ambitions drove them on year after year, while self-doubts were never far below the surface. Robert Keayne, the wealthy Boston merchant of the early period, built a fine fortune, but at great cost. When censured by the clergy for acting against the public good, he was crushed and, in a document written to clear himself of guilt, poured out the tensions he had long felt.

Throughout the seventeenth century a few Puritans experienced Keayne's miseries, but the temptations of worldly pride were too remote to hurt the consciences of most. The opportunities for gain were largely inaccessible to ordinary men until after 1690, when economic expansion opened new prospects to many more farmers and merchants. Common men could take up a small trade or invest in a ship sailing to the West Indies, and land purchased in a new plantation doubled in value within a few years. The expansive economy of the early eighteenth century unleashed ambitions restrained by the absence of opportunity. Everyone hoped to prosper; the demand for land banks and the 300 percent increase in per capita indebtedness were measures of the eagerness for wealth. An indentured farmhand in the 1740's complained that his master never spoke about religion: "His whole attention was taken up on the pursuits of the good things of this world; wealth was his supreme object. I am afraid gold was his God."

In the midst of this economic growth, the ministers faithfully excoriated the spreading worldliness. It was obvious, one minister wrote, "that the Heart of a People is gone off from God and gone after the Creature; that they are much more concerned about getting Land and Money and Stock, than they be about getting Religion revived." "The Concern is not as heretofore to accommodate themselves as to the Worship of God," it was said in 1730, "but Where they can have most Land, and be under best advantages to get Money." These accusations were put aside with the usual rationalizations, but so long as the ministers reminded men that riches cankered their souls, a grave uncertainty haunted everyone who pursued wealth.

The desire to prosper also precipitated clashes with law and authority, adding to accumulating guilt. With increasing frequency after 1690 people fought their rulers or balked at the

laws, usually as a consequence of their ambition. Such friction
wore away confidence as it convinced men inwardly of their own
culpability.

Under more peaceful circumstances law and authority pro-
tected the Puritan from the asperities of his own doctrines.
Taken seriously, Puritan theology kept men in unbearable sus-
pense about their standing with God: He chose whom He would
to be saved, and the rest were cast into the fires of hell. But the
founding fathers had qualified this pure conception of divine
sovereignty by stressing the authority vested in the social order.
Since civil and ecclesiastical rulers were commissioned by God
and the laws of society were an expression of His will, obedience
to Connecticut's government was in effect obedience to divine
government, and the good will of the rulers was an omen of God's
good will. So long as man complied with the law and submitted
to authority, he was safe from divine punishment.

After 1690, in their ambition to prosper, people disregarded
the demands of social order. Nonproprietors contested the control of town lands with proprietors, and outlivers struggled with
the leaders in the town center to obtain an independent parish.
In the civil government settlers fought for a clear title to their
lands and new traders for currency. Church members resisted
the enlargement of the minister's power or demanded greater
piety in his preaching. All these controversies pitted common
men against rulers and the laws.

Under these circumstances the social order became a menace
to peace of mind rather than a shield against divine wrath. Just
as conformity gave an inward assurance of moral worth, so resistance, even in spirit, was blameworthy. Dissenters, in politics
or economics as well as religion, could not oppose the community
fathers whom God had set to rule without feeling guilty. Even
when a move to the outlands or complaints about a minister's
arrogance were well justified, the participants in the action feared
that they sinned in resisting.

Few men in 1740 were outright rebels, for strong loyalties
still bound almost all to their communities. By comparison to
their forebears of 1690, however, this later generation was
estranged. It could not comfort itself in the recollection of a

life of conformity to the divinely sanctioned order. In part it was emboldened by the wealth it had sought and often gained, but that provided an unsteady support when the pursuit of riches was so often condemned. However hardened the contentious appeared, guilt generated by an undue love of wealth and by resistance to the social order had hollowed out their lives.

East of the Connecticut River, in the most rapidly expanding section of the colony, turmoil was greatest. Extravagant growth plunged the towns into strife over land titles, currency, and religion. The party battles loosened the social structure and alienated men from their social and religious leaders. Economic opportunity also aroused the hunger for land and commercial success. Here the revival was noticeably most intense. "Whatever be the reason," Ezra Stiles commented later, "the eastern part of Connecticut . . . are of a very mixt and uncertain character as to religion. Exhorters, Itinerants, Separate Meetings rose in that part." Around three-quarters of the separations between 1740 and 1755 occurred east of the Connecticut River. The greatest number in any town—four—were in Norwich, the commercial center of the east. Nearby towns—New London, Groton, Stonington, Lyme, Windham, and Preston—had similarly prospered, and a third of the separations in the colony took place in these towns and Norwich. These departures, roughly measuring the fervor of the Awakening, were the outcome of the personal instability eastern men felt after a half-century of extraordinary expansion.

Before Whitefield arrived, ministers sensed the shaky state of their parishioners' confidence. One pastor noted the grave uncertainty of people under spiritual concern: "They want to know they shall be sure they believe, that they love God, that they are in the right way, are sincere and the like." As the ministers recognized, an outward show usually covered somber doubts: reprobates disguised or fled from their real condition while inwardly they suffered from a consciousness of guilt.

Whitefield broke through this facade. Though he stood apart from the established clergy, he was accepted by them. He did not represent the repressive ministerial rule which entered so largely into the conflicts of the period but nevertheless came

clothed with acknowledged authority. The revivals he started in
the middle colonies also imbued him with a reputation of extraordinary power. "Hearing how god was with him every where as
he came along," one awakened person later reported, "it solum-
nized my mind and put me in a trembling fear before he began to
preach for he looked as if he was Cloathed with authority from
the great god." Besides, he was an impassioned and fluent
preacher.

Whitefield moved his hearers because excessive worldliness
and resistance to the divinely sanctioned social order had already
undermined their confidence. He told men what they already
knew subconsciously: that they had broken the law, that impulses beyond their control drove them to resist divine authority,
and that outward observance did not signify loving and willing
submission. Confronted with truth, his listeners admitted that
they were "vile, unworthy, loathsom" wretches. "Hearing him
preach," a converted man said, "gave me a heart wound. By
gods blessing my old foundation was broken up and i saw that
my righteousness would not save me."

This confrontation of guilt, the first part of conversion, drove
men to despair, but the revivalists did not leave their hearers
there to suffer. By publicly identifying the sources of guilt and
condemning them, the preachers also helped to heal the wounds
they first inflicted. Converts were persuaded that by acknowl-
edging and repudiating their old sins, they were no longer cul-
pable. The reborn man was as joyful and loving when the process
was completed as he was miserable at its start.

Converts were told, for instance, that wealth held no attrac-
tions for the saintly. The business of Christ's disciples, one
preacher taught, "is not to hunt for Riches, and Honours, and
Pleasures in this World, but to despise them, and deny themselves, and be ready to part with even all the lawful Pleasures
and Comforts of the World at any Time." In a dramatic gesture
expressing a deep impulse, Davenport had his followers gather
the symbols of worldliness—wigs, cloaks, hoods, gowns, rings,
necklaces—into a heap and burn them.

Converts responded eagerly, casting off with great relief their
guilt-producing ambition. The pious David Brainerd spontan-
eously broke into poetry:

Farewell, vain world; my soul can bid Adieu:
My Saviour's taught me to abandon you.

After Isaac Backus[14] was converted, he felt that he "should not be troubled any more with covetousness. The earth and all that is therein appeared to be vanity." His mother, also a convert, felt ready to "give up my name, estate, family, life and breath, freely to God." She would not relinquish her peace of soul "no, not to be in the most prosperous condition in temporal things that ever I was in." For many the choice was to enjoy peace of soul or prosperity. The pursuit of wealth and an easy conscience were incompatible. Jonathan Edwards noted a temptation among converts to go to extremes and "to neglect worldly affairs too much." They were unwilling to jeopardize their new-found peace by returning to worldliness.

The revivalists undermined the social order, the other main source of guilt, not by repudiating law and authority, but by denying them sanctifying power. Estrangement from rulers and the traditional patterns of life was demoralizing as long as the social order was considered divine, but Awakening preachers repeatedly denied that salvation came by following the law. No amount of covenant owning, Sabbath observance, moral rectitude, or obedience to rulers redeemed the soul. Praying, Bible study, and attendance at worship might result solely from worldly motives, to avoid disgrace or to pacify a guilty conscience. "Civility and external Acts belonging to Morality," one revivalist taught, "are no Part of the Essence of the Religion of Christ." Without grace, "tho men are adorn'd with many amiable qualities, and lead sober, regular, and to all appearance religious lives, yet they remain under the condemning sentence of the Law, and perish at last in a state of unsanctified nature." Reborn men were expected to practice moral virtues, but their salvation was not at stake. Obedience brought no assurance of grace, and disobedience did not entail damnation. Though still driven to resist rulers or to depart from the ap-

---

[14] A prominent Connecticut New Light separatist and ultimately the most crucial figure of the early Baptist movement.

proved pattern of community life, believers in the revival message felt little guilt.

In this fashion the Awakening cleared the air of tensions. Men admitted that they had lusted after wealth, condemned themselves for it, and afterwards walked with lighter hearts. They ended the long struggle with the social order by denying its power to save and hence to condemn. After a century of Puritan rule, law and authority were burdens too heavy to bear. All the anxiety they evoked was released when men grasped the idea that salvation came not by obedience to law.

In the converts' minds the escape from guilt was possible because of God's grace. The idea that the law could not condemn if God justified contained the deepest meaning of the Awakening. The rules and rulers, who governed both externally and in the conscience, had judged men and found them wanting until God out of His good grace suspended the sentence of damnation. The authority of Christ nullified earthly authority. Edwards said that converted men exulted that "God is self-sufficient, and infinitely above all dependence, and reigns over all." In the inward struggle with guilt, God's infinite power overruled the older authority that had stood over every Puritan conscience, judging and condemning.

In that moment of grace the Awakening worked its revolution. Henceforth a personal relation with God governed the reborn men who were empowered by faith to obey the God they knew personally above the divine will manifest in earthly law and authority. It was characteristic of the converted to "renounce all confidence in everything but Christ, and build all their hopes of happiness upon this unalterable Rock of Ages." "I seemed to depend wholly on my dear Lord," Brainerd reported following his conversion. "God was so precious to my soul that the world with all its enjoyments was infinitely vile. I had no more value for the favor of men than for pebbles. The Lord was my ALL." Though the old authority was still a substantial force in every life, it did not structure the identity of converts as much as their own bright picture of God.

Under the government of this personal, internal authority, converts experienced a peace and joy unknown under earthly fathers and their old conscience. God's grace dissolved uncertainty and fear. The convert testified to the "sweet solace, rest and joy of soul," the image of God bestowed. "The thought of having so great, so glorious, and excellent a Being for his Father, his Friend, and his Home, sets his heart at Ease from all his anxious Fears and Distresses." The power to replace oppressive authority figures with faith in a loving God was the ultimate reason for the revivalists' success.

Thus the men affected by the Awakening possessed a new character, cleansed of guilt and joyful in the awareness of divine favor. Unfortunately for the social order, however, their personal redemption did not save society. In making peace with themselves, converts inwardly revolted against the old law and authority, and, as time was to show, they would eventually refuse to submit to a social order alien to their new identity. Conservative suspicions of the revival were confirmed when reborn men set out to create a new society compatible with the vision opened in the Great Awakening.

22   Dietmar Rothermund
The Americanization of Denominations

Dietmar Rothermund, a German exchange scholar studying at the University of Pennsylvania at the time he first wrote on the Great Awakening, views it also as part of a process of Americanization, pointing to the assault on authority and, more emphatically, the denominational structure that appeared. His setting is Pennsylvania, but his generalizations—developed more fully in his The Laymen's Progress: Religious and Political Experience in Colonial Pennsylvania, 1740–1770 *(Philadelphia, 1961)—can be applied everywhere.*

SOURCE. Dietmar Rothermund, "Political Factions and the Great Awakening," *Pennsylvania History*, XXVI, 1959, pp. 317–331. Reprinted by permission of the publisher and the author.

The Great Awakening began as an interdenominational revival of religion and ended in an invigorated denominational
consciousness. The different denominations entered this spiritual
whirlpool with enthusiasm or skepticism, and left it elated or
alarmed; passing through it they changed their relationship to
each other. Indifference became partisanship and affinities grew
into alliances. . . . The Great Awakening was started by . . .
religious leaders but it ended in making the layman the supreme
judge in ecclesiastical matters. It was the layman who threw the
"unconverted" or the "unorthodox" minister out of the church,
according to his own judgment as to his conversion or orthodoxy.
In this situation the minister could no longer command or order;
he had to manipulate and agitate. If he was imperious or un-
inspiring, he soon found himself without support.

Out of these developments grew a specifically American experience. The encounter of denominations . . . and the awakening of the layman produced a new climate which affected the
European heritage of all denominations. Parts of this European
heritage entered into the new experience, but it was the interaction of these elements in the Great Awakening which became
for all denominations the foundation for their common American
heritage. This interaction forced the denominations to look at
each other—be it in admiration or disgust—rather than back at
the fathers in Europe. In this way a curious combination of old
and new feuds, old and new allegiances emerged, and the sum
of this new experience was very different from its original parts.

In Pennsylvania this development was especially interesting
because not only the English groups but also many German
groups participated in the process of Americanization. In order
to understand what happened to these groups in the Great
Awakening, we have to examine their background and their
relationships to each other in Europe and later in America.

There is a basic conflict in Christianity between religious
experience and religious organization. Religious experience at its
best penetrates the individual soul and connects it with eternity.
Religious organization is a temporal union of believers for matters of worship, common dogma, and the teaching of the Gospel
to coming generations. Ideally experience and organization sup-

plement each other, because even the soul experiencing eternity has to live in a temporal world. However, in numerous cases religious experience has threatened to dissolve religious organization, and as frequently religious organization has tended to stifle religious experience. In most of these situations, movements have been started which broke away from their contemporary religious organizations. A movement derives its energy from a sense of urgency, and it is difficult to keep up this feeling for more than one generation. Consequently such a movement either vanishes, or perpetuates itself in the form of a sect.

Up to the time of the Reformation the Catholic Church avoided this conflict by allowing individual mystics, and numerous religious orders a degree of freedom within its own ranks. The Protestant churches, however, themselves born of a religious movement, permitted no such freedom and left only the possibilities of dissent and secession. Consequently the period of the Reformation saw the rise of a number of movements which became sects or, in a few cases, new churches—and every generation since the Reformation has added to the number.

The authority on which dissent and secession were founded has always claimed direct access to revelation, either from within through an "inner light," or from without through reliance on the Bible pure and simple. Thus, a great number of Inspirationist or Biblicist sects sprang up all over Europe. This scattering of believers led necessarily to some serious thinking, and a consensus that if revelation is meaningful it has to be one, and obviously many particular claims to revelation must be spurious. From this insight arose the idea of "the community of God in the Spirit."

During the 17th century two plans for such a community became prominent: the idea called "Philadelphia," and the idea of the "ecclesiola in ecclesia ['little church in The Church']." "Philadelphia"—literally, fraternal love—meant a spiritual union of true believers, whatever their outward rank or denomination might be. At first "Philadelphia" was nothing but a program. With persecution and distress, however, a new solidarity grew up, and "Philadelphia" was thought of more and more as a place of refuge. On the continent tolerant princes could offer their own estates as a "Philadelphia" for religious seekers of all kinds. In England the new colonial expansion offered a way out, and it was in keeping with the spirit of the time that a new proprietor of Pennsylvania, William Penn, named his colonial capital Philadelphia. However, Philadelphia depended on the inspiration and experience of its founders and defied institutional organization. Therefore the movement could not survive once the experience was lost, and the founders were dead. The community remained but the spirit changed. The "ecclesiola" had a similar fate. It started as a kind of Protestant alternative to the Catholic orders, as movements within the church. Church and movement, experience and organization should remain together, the movement should be the leaven of the church, the ecclesiola should be the motor of the ecclesia; these were the ideals of the pietists who met in conventicles all over the continent. The vigor of this movement waned after a few decades, but the foment had indeed leavened the church.

A unique attempt to combine all the ideals of pietism was made by Count Zinzendorf. He had been a pietist at one time, and a Philadelphian at another; he tried to form an ecclesiola with his Order of the Mustard Seed. Unlike many other advocates of religious experience he had a deep interest in the church as a community, and as a preserver of the means of grace. Therefore he tried to establish a movement-church, which combined the vigor of the movement with the stability of the church.

The need to keep church and movement together was urgently and universally felt in the period from 1730 to 1740. The English Methodism of John Wesley was a response to the same needs which Zinzendorf had seen in his own country. However, while Wesley considered himself a member of the Anglican church throughout his life, Zinzendorf had to face a more difficult problem. The Lutheran Church of which Zinzendorf considered himself a member was only one of the churches and sects which he wanted to reach with his message of the "community of God in the Spirit." Therefore he devised a complicated scheme of ecumenical organization. He molded the ancient Moravian

Church, to some of whose refugees he had granted asylum on his estates, into a "community of God in the Spirit." Then he joined to this church, in the form of autonomous departments, groups of believers of the Lutheran and Reformed Churches who wanted to cooperate with him. He supplied this unique organization with a theology based on the atonement or, as it was termed by him, "the blood of the Lamb."

The ecumenical intentions of Zinzendorf's program were not universally appreciated, and his enemies accused him of deliberate ambiguities. Yet as a missionary organization his "community of God in the Spirit" became an immediate success. Within his lifetime the dynamic Count controlled a world-wide network of missions and sent scores of dedicated revivalists to many parts of the globe. Although Zinzendorf wanted to remain a member of the Lutheran Church, the very momentum of his organization separated him from this church. In this respect his movement had a different history from that of Methodism, which needed a second generation to develop into a distinct organization.

The English parallel to Zinzendorf was George Whitefield. This great revivalist had many of the same characteristics: an occasional rashness of judgment, tireless energy, impatience, an ecumenical spirit, and oratorical gifts, but he did not share Zinzendorf's concern about a theology of atonement, nor his preoccupation with church organization. His revivalist appeal and his indifference to doctrinal subtleties made Whitefield as popular with the dissenters as with the Anglican masses. Most dissenters, Presbyterians and others, actually needed him as much as the Anglicans did, because dissent had become nearly as stiff an establishment as the Established Church itself.

In America the spiritual situation in the eighteenth century was in many respects similar to the one in Europe, but the problem was aggravated by a tendency to meet the challenges of a new environment by clinging obstinately to standards that were valid "at home." This tendency was most apparent in the attitude toward the ordination of ministers in America. Ordination is a central feature of a church, and a constant source of suspicion and scorn to a movement. No church can exist with-

out a standard pattern of recruiting and installing ministers, and
no movement will accept the fact that a minister merely by
virtue of ordination becomes an authentic messenger of God.

The education and ordination of an indigenous American
clergy was one of the major steps toward the emancipation of
America from European tutelage. But in America itself sectarian
apprehensions and the conservatism of many older ministers
stood against this development.

The Biblicist and Inspirationist sects of Pennsylvania had no
formal problems with regard to the recruiting of religious leadership within their own ranks. They viewed the churches' re-
cruitment with suspicion because an increase of ordained ministers meant to them the danger of a new establishment, and
with it the possibility of renewed persecution. Church members in Pennsylvania, however, had to depend on the churches
in their home countries for a supply of new ministers. But no
minister who was not either an ardent idealist or a man with a
dubious record at home could be persuaded to come to Pennsylvania, unless a fixed salary and traveling expenses were guar-
anteed. Local education and ordination of an American clergy
might have solved this problem, but there were numerous obstacles. Educational opportunities in America were limited and
the right to ordain ministers was vested in higher church authorities, who for the most part resided on the other side of
the ocean, and had little knowledge of American affairs. If
there were to be higher church authorities in America, more
ministers were needed—and that completed the vicious circle.
Thus, increasingly the Anglicans looked to the Bishop of London, the Presbyterians to the Church of Scotland, the Reformed
Church to the Classis of Amsterdam, and the Lutherans to the
University of Halle and the Lutheran Court Preacher of King
George for their supply of ministers.

The constitution of the Presbyterian Church was perhaps the
best for handling this situation and for breaking through this
dependence on Europe. Any properly organized presbytery could
ordain ministers. There were several presbyteries in America
by 1740, and there was even a well-organized synod of these
presbyteries, but the ministers belonging to the presbyteries were

conservative and hesitated to ordain anyone who did not have a European education. Because of the scarcity of such an education among possible candidates in America the presbyteries guarded their standards the more jealously. In spite of the advantages of their constitution, the Presbyterians too looked to Europe.

A small group in the Presbyterian Church, mainly consisting of the Tennent family, had tried to break the deadlock by establishing a "Log College" for the local education of ministers. William Tennent, the founder of the college, was a convert to Presbyterianism, who had left the Established Church of Ireland because he disliked "the usurped power of bishops" and the "connivance of the church at the practice of Arminian doctrines." His colleagues in the Presbyterian synod, however, were mostly conservatives who did not trust the "Log College" men.

This was the situation when George Whitefield, and Zinzendorf's Moravians, came to Pennsylvania. Whitefield started a revival of religion in Philadelphia which marked the high point of the Great Awakening in Pennsylvania.[15] His own Anglican Church noted the revival with embarrassment. Commissioner Cummings, the representative of the Bishop of London, preached against Whitefield. But it was not the Anglican Church which felt the greatest impact of the Great Awakening—it was the Presbyterian Church. Gilbert Tennent joined the revival and preached a vigorous sermon on the dangers of an unconverted ministry. This was no longer a revival, but a revolt. The Log College men turned the tables on the representatives of the Presbyterian organization and pitted the converted heart against European education as the hallmark of ministry. When this revolutionary doctrine invaded the church, a split was inevitable. From Tennent's sermon both ministers and laymen had to assume that an awakened soul could pass judgment on the state of conversion of ministers, and that while a minister was bound

---

[15] In Rothermund's terminology, "revival" denotes the period of Whitefield's first itineracy in 1740; "Great Awakening" denotes a broader revival lasting, in Pennsylvania, from 1740 to 1748.

to his people, the people were as free from their minister after an official call as before. The Presbyterian conservatives were appalled by this subversive idea, and in 1741 the Synod of Philadelphia excluded the Log College men. The latter immediately formed a presbytery of their own, and took it upon themselves to ordain ministers who conformed to their standards. Thus, the deadlock was broken, and converts of the Whitefield revival were gathered into the fold of New Light Presbyterianism.

The next revolution in the ordination of ministers came with the arrival of Moravian bishops in Pennsylvania. Under Zinzendorf's plan these bishops could ordain not only Moravian ministers but also Lutheran and Reformed ministers. As a movement-church the Moravian Church of Zinzendorf did not insist on education for the ministry but would ordain any awakened soul. The revival of religion which Zinzendorf and his Moravians brought about among the Germans in Pennsylvania was in many respects more successful than the revival which Whitefield and the New Light Presbyterians had brought about among the English. Missionaries came in great numbers in a ship owned by the Moravian Church, and within a few months there was hardly a German community in Pennsylvania which had not been visited by a preacher of Zinzendorf's following.

In the beginning the two movements worked together. Whitefield had been deeply influenced by the Moravians. The year 1740, however, saw a multiple split in what had been a more or less united front. In July, 1740, Wesley parted company with the Moravians in London, because of their excessive religious enthusiasm. Moreover, at about the same time the Calvinist Methodists developed into a separate group and Whitefield, who had become under the tutelage of Gilbert Tennent considerably more Calvinist in his ministry, joined with the Calvinist Methodists and severed his connections with Wesley's group. In November, 1740, when Whitefield came back to Pennsylvania, he precipitated a heated doctrinal debate with the Moravian theologian, Peter Boehler, who had had a strong influence on Wesley. Whitefield insisted on predestination; Boehler emphasized salvation by the Blood of the Lamb, that is, the redeeming power of the atonement. After this clash the united front was dissolved in America, too. . . . The conflict which thus arose was the beginning of a heightened denominational conscious- ness in Pennsylvania. The rejection of revivalism by the Old Side Presbyterians and the Anglicans, and by the quietist sects, contributed even more to this increase in denominational self- awareness. The days of interdenominational enthusiasm had been only a brief interlude.

The New Light Presbyterians quickly consolidated their church organization. In 1745 the Synod of New York was formed by the Presbyteries of New Brunswick and New York; in 1749 the first overtures toward a reunion with the Old Side Synod of Philadelphia were made. The Moravian Church, how- ever, spread itself too thin. In the interest of the Awakening an interdenominational activity was kept up on a grand scale. A vast area was supplied with ministers, and yet no congrega- tion thus served was asked to assume the status of a Moravian congregation. The Moravians went out of their way to avoid the charge of being proselytizers. From 1741 to 1748 they tried to maintain the spirit of the Seven Pennsylvania Synods,[16] and it was not until 1748 that the first general synod of the Moravian Church was held.

At that conference the Moravians decided on a new system of ordination and made it known to all who wanted to be served by Moravian missionaries that they would have to move to places where a regular Moravian community could be es- tablished. This meant the abandonment of an interdenomina- tional service, and a disciplined consolidation of the Moravian Church as one denomination among others. The consolidation of the Moravian Church in America was thus a rather late event. A few years earlier, at the height of Moravian revivalist work (1742–45), a great many converts might have joined the Moravian Church. By the time of the consolidation, however, vigorous competition as well as Moravian reluctance to appear as proselytizers, had lessened the ranks of prospective converts.

One of the most decisive elements in the situation was the persistence of Zinzendorf's old adversaries at Halle University and in London, who saw to it that an energetic Lutheran min-

---

[16] Interdenominational synods held in 1741–1742.

ister was sent to America to challenge the Moravian missions
to the Lutherans. Henry Melchior Muhlenberg, the Lutheran
minister who was sent to Pennsylvania by Dr. G. A. Francke of
Halle with recommendations by the Lutheran Court Preacher
in London, arrived in Philadelphia in 1742, two years after
Whitefield's revival, and one year after the arrival of Count Zinzendorf in Philadelphia. The short period of time between Zinzendorf's arrival and Muhlenberg's had been enough for the
Moravians to penetrate most Lutheran congregations. Zinzendorf himself served as a Lutheran minister in Philadelphia.
Naturally Muhlenberg faced an uphill task. He had to reclaim
the Lutheran congregations from the Moravians, and he had to
take over from Zinzendorf in Philadelphia. Moreover, he had
to guard himself against the attacks of German sectarians who
had an aversion against any church man, be he Zinzendorf or
Muhlenberg.

Undoubtedly a staid minister of an established church would
have hesitated to take up such a work. But Muhlenberg was a
Halle Pietist, a missionary who had been preparing to go to
India when his instructions were changed and he was sent to
Pennsylvania. . . . Muhlenberg's missionary zeal curbed the
influence of the Moravian Church. However, he had to spend
years in America before his influence outweighed that of the
Moravians. His attempts to organize a Lutheran synod, thereby
establishing a Lutheran Church authority in America, were frus-
trated for some years by Moravian resistance.

The first overtures toward Lutheran Church unity and organization had been made by laymen. The Swedish merchant Peter
Kock had been eager to bring about a union of all Lutheran
ministers and congregations, Swedish as well as German. He
invited all ministers to a synodal meeting in 1745. There seems
to have been a plan to elect Muhlenberg as president of the
synod at that time. However, the Swedish Lutheran minister,
Laurentius Nyberg, who adhered to the Moravian leadership
and who also attended this meeting obstructed this plan. Among
other things he insisted Peter Kock had no right to call ministers to a synod, since Kock was a layman. In the months after
this abortive synod, Laurentius Nyberg made an attempt to

attach the Swedish to the Moravian interest—an attempt which caused much alarm and misunderstanding among the German Lutherans. Finally, the Archbishop of Upsala sent a testimony against Nyberg to Pennsylvania, in 1747, and deprived him of his credentials as a Lutheran minister. Nyberg then joined the Moravian church. Only after these obstacles had been overcome, could Muhlenberg found a German Lutheran synod. At this synod—in August, 1748—Muhlenberg and his colleagues for the first time ordained a Lutheran minister in America. . . .

By 1748 the Great Awakening had reached its final stage; the first period of revivalism had given way to a period of realignment of denominations, and this period had been followed by a third period, the period of consolidation and organization along American lines. New denominational synods had been created, new plans for education were under way. . . .

Through partisanship and controversy the American churches had finally come into their own. Indigenous church authorities now ordained locally educated ministers, and American religious organizations were beginning to stand as equals to their European counterparts. A state of dependence was changing to a relationship of mutual consultation. At the same time the intensive participation of the layman in church affairs, which became one of the most outstanding features of American religious life, was initiated in these years, when laymen seconded their ministers, founded synods, and listened to numerous speakers who tried to win their souls for one cause or another. The existence of the various denominations, aligned in numerous ways, made it necessary for each of them to tolerate the others and to live together with religious and political opponents. . . .

23 FROM *Leonard J. Trinterud*
The New Light Snuffed Out

In making their exuberant claim for a cardinal place in the evolution of an American mind for the Great Awakening, some historians have—in the view of other historians—tended to forget the intellectual and institutional course followed by New Light and New Side ministers. Critics point out that in New England, New Light doctrine gave way to an almost incomprehensible New Divinity and the heirs of Jonathan Edwards became so recondite as to lose their congregations altogether. With regard to the Middle Colonies, Leonard J. Trinterud, the foremost historian of the origins of Presbyterianism, has followed the logic of New Light preaching and found it ultimately all but indistinguishable from the rational Old Light. One can similarly follow New Light and New Side institutions and find them ultimately—to borrow Rothermund's words—"as stiff establishments" as any of the pre-Awakening establishments, differing from their predecessors only in their separation from the state.

The salvation of sinners was not to be found in their welfare, but in their restoration to the service of God. Few emphases were as uncompromisingly made in the New Side preaching as was this consistent and vigorous denial of any and all notions of eudaemonism. The nature of the Christian life was accordingly the service of God, not any form of religious experience psychologically interpreted. Neither did the notion of the value of one's religious experience for the individual play any role. In the most blunt terms it was declared that man existed for God's purposes. Hence behind all this thought on regeneration stood at all times its unquestioned presuppositions, the doctrines of the sovereignty of God, and his predestination.

SOURCE. Leonard J. Trinterud, *The Forming of an American Tradition: A Re-examination of Colonial Presbyterianism.* Philadelphia: The Westminister Press, pp. 191–195. Copyright 1949 by W. L. Jenkins. Used by permission.

Good works were indeed required of the Christian, but not because they changed God's purposes and designs toward the doer, or excited his benevolence. Neither were they to be done because they in any way qualified one to receive Christ, nor because that by doing them sanctification would be furthered, nor in hopes that God would give further grace for further growth in grace. Good works were necessary because "they are one End of our Election," because they are part of sanctification itself, because they are done as an expression of obedience to God, and, because they are an expression of gratitude to God, an evidence of reality of faith, and an aid to assurance. He who does not have good works ought not to pretend to be converted. "An unjust, uncharitable Christian is as great a contradiction as a prayerless, or a swearing Christian. You can no more be a good man without loving your neighbor, than without loving your God. . . . No inward experience, no religious duties, no zeal in devotion can make you true Christians." "Men seem to act as if they were entirely detached from one another, and had no connection, or were not at all concerned to promote each other's interest. Self-interest is their pursuit, and self-love their ruling passion." The good as such, in God's sight, was possible only through grace. Christian morality differed from natural morality in that it was done in obedience to God's command, and done in the name of Christ. Ethical good in general was "rectitude of a reasonable creature, or conformity to rule and law." Christian morality was morality that conformed to Christian norms. Christian obedience was the obedience that God enabled man to perform.

The controlling note . . . accordingly, had always been the concept of law. This note is regnant in all the Log College literature, and in the writings of all colonial Presbyterians. "The Moral Law, as to its Substance, is the same with the Law of Nature, which is immutable, and founded in the reasonable Nature of Man," Gilbert Tennent declared. "By the Law of Nature I understand the Light of Nature, or the practical Notions of the Difference between Moral Good and Evil, which we receive with our Nature; or a practical Rule of Moral Duties, which was originally impress'd on the human Mind when Man was first form'd to which Mankind are by Nature oblig'd. Altho' this Law of Nature was much broken by the Fall of Man, yet that there be some Remains of it in all, we have abundant Evidence from Scripture, Conscience, the Consent of Mankind, and the Voice of Reason." This law is "co-natural" to man, and was engraven upon his heart at creation. "Things that are Moral are commanded because they are intrinsically Good, and agreeable to that eternal Justice and Goodness that are in God Himself."

The fall of man so far darkened man's understanding, will, and affections that a "second edition" of this moral law was needed. This second edition was given in the Ten Command-ments. The Decalogue was accordingly the best summary of this natural law, or moral law of love to God and neighbor. The Golden Rule itself fell into this same category. "This [that is, the Golden Rule], says our Lord, is the Law and the Prophets, i.e., It is the Substance of the second Table of the Law, according to the Explication thereof by the Prophets: The Law is just and reasonable, grounded upon the plainest Maxims of natural Equity and Right." The example of Jesus was the best possible explication of this law of love, but since, as the Bible records it, it is fragmentary and does not cover all cir-cumstances of life, the law as summarized in the Decalogue is also needed for completeness' sake.

During the most vigorous phase of the revival, and again dur-ing the controversy with the Moravians, this conviction that the law applied equally to Christian and non-Christian was force-fully asserted. "Christ is not exalted, but dishonour'd and the Interest of his Kingdom betray'd, while any that assume the Character of his Ambassadors neglect to inculcate the Moral Law." That the Moravians denied that the law was any longer a rule for the Christian was denounced as one of their most serious errors. An individualistic piety, or any notion that only Christians made for righteousness in society, was rejected. The assumption was that society was in some measure Christian, and that the function of the Church was to make it more so. This attitude was very plain in all New Side preaching. All their hearers were in some measure committed to be Christians, society in general was so committed, and so also were all the institutions of society—governments, courts, schools, and all others.

The Christian, while obligated to obey this law of love, did so in a manner different from that of the non-Christian. The former obeyed it because of a sense of gratitude to God and without any thought of obtaining any merit or reward. The non-Christian obeyed through fear and with hopes of reward. The Christian remained, however, both flesh and spirit, and, accordingly, never obeyed the law fully. Neither did he ever reach the stage of growth in which his obedience became natural, or could be assumed. In so far as he was aided by the Holy Spirit through grace, the spirit, or the new man, would triumph. In so far as sin prevailed, the flesh triumphed. The warfare between these two principles, the flesh and the spirit, or the old man and the new, continued throughout life, and determined the nature of man's obedience to God. Though regenerated, justified, and living by faith, man remained both sinner and justified believer. "The more holy a Person is," Gilbert Tennent declared in the midst of the revival period, "the more they know of themselves. The Knowledge of God is that Glass in which they behold their own Blemishes, the secret Corruptions of their hearts, the Sins of their Practice, and the Defects of their Religious Service." A continual renewal of repentance was therefore utterly essential. "The evidences of pardon and the hope of salvation do not put an end to true repentance, but, on the other hand, promote it." "Evangelical repentance does not consist in despairing agonies and hopeless horrors of conscience, but is attended with an humble hope of forgiveness and acceptance; and this hope is founded entirely upon the merits of Jesus, and not of our repentance and reformation."

Against such a background it is not surprising to find that in discussion of the nature of communion with God, the element most stressed was obedience and not love, righteousness and not joy. The emotional aspects of communion with God were not of the essence of true communion, but obedience was. Moreover, it was in the stated ordinances of worship that communion was best to be found. The constant longing for the emotional aspects was a sign of immaturity. An excellent illustration of this sense of obedience as the keynote of Christian living is to be found in a conversation between Whitefield and William Tennent, II, when the latter was an old man. Whitefield, whose soul was ravished at the thought of dying, asked Tennent if he did not feel the same joy. Tennent, generally reputed by his contemporaries to be the most "heavenly-minded" of all the Log College men, replied: "No, sir, it is no pleasure to me at all; and, if you knew your duty, it would be none to you. I have nothing to do with death. My business is to live as long as I can, and as well as I can. . . . I am God's servant, and have engaged to do His business as long as He pleases to continue me therein."

This thrusting of obedience to the forefront of the Christian life had its influence upon the whole character of New Side preaching and teaching during the revival and subsequently. The Christian was not to flee the sinful society about him, but to lay hold of it and bring it into at least some degree of conformity to the will of God. In so doing he was to co-operate with whatever forces would work with him. No area of life fell outside the realms that God controlled and desired to use for his own purposes. Consequently wherever the Christian's work found him in that vocation he was to serve God. To be without "Publick Spirit" was to be without God. "Unless you conscientiously observe the duties of social life, you cannot enter the kingdom of heaven." Such duties were those incident to the assumption of a responsible part in the normal functions of society. Out of this conviction came the interest of the New Side in education, in civil government, and in all public affairs. "Brethren, we were born not merely for ourselves, but the Publick Good! which as Members of Society we are obliged *pro virili* to promote."

Both New Side and Old Side, evangelical and rationalist, emerged, therefore, at the same point—obedience to God's eternal law, the natural law of man's reason and conscience, was the essence of the Christian life. Federalism had always led to this conclusion. Moralism and complacency were inevitable, accordingly, whenever the rationalistic element dominated.

Even license had then appeared. For a time the New Side had been able to combat this inherent weakness of the Federal system by reintroducing the Puritan pilgrimage motif, and the Puritan doctrines of convictions and assurance. In this context it had again become possible to bring the more evangelical aspects of the Puritan understanding of the Christian life to the fore. The Great Awakening within colonial Presbyterianism had been wholly shaped by this evangelical emphasis. Gradually, however, the rationalistic core . . . was to reassert itself, and come to virtually unchallenged supremacy as the century drew to a close. The New Light was snuffed out.

24   J. M. Bumsted
The Stable Context of Americanization

If the selections thus far, and particularly those from the works of Perry Miller and Alan Heimert, represent one thrust of scholarship—call it macrohistory in that it deals with great themes slashed through the past—J. M. Bumsted represents another, the slow building toward themes by painstaking analysis of individuals and communities—call it, for convenience, microhistory. The techniques of microhistory, as Bumsted applied them to Norwich, Connecticut, tend to indicate that the Awakening per se was not a cataclysmic force for Americanization (in terms of the assault on the traditional order), but merely a part of a broader process. A matter of convenience for some and of Awakening doctrine for others, led men in Norwich to desire separation from the established Congregational church, hence to challenge the authority of that church. And if it was no more than a matter of convenience for some, that fact would constitute a caveat against any generalization made thus far as to the effect of the Awakening on the American mind. For all the generalizations are drawn from the writings

SOURCE. J. M. Bumsted, "Revivalism and Separatism in New England: The First Society of Norwich, Connecticut, as a Case Study," *William and Mary Quarterly*, Ser. 3, XXIV, 1967, pp. 588–593, 599–603, 605–612. Reprinted by permission of the Institute of Early American History and Culture and the author.

and sermons of intellectual figures, and one is bound to ask whether
the ordinary men of the past—whose individual minds in toto must
constitute the mind—were as assiduous and impressionable readers as
the historians who have looked back on the past. The question Bumsted
implicitly raises is basic: How is the historian to understand the re-
lationship of ideas and actions?

After 1740, New England's religious and ecclesiastical life
became increasingly disordered by schism, separations, and the
ultimate rise of new religious denominations. The upheaval was
caused in part by the introduction of a new and radical pietism
into the thinking of large numbers of converts of the Great
Awakening, which led them to reject many religious and ecclesiastical practices common in the established churches of New
England. The analyses and explanations of the nature and
strength of the pietistic impulse produced by the revival are full
and impressive. In the hands of a recent generation of historians, the evangelical aspect of the Awakening has received
a sympathetic and understanding treatment, and no one can
doubt or question its great significance. What has been frequently overlooked, however, in attempting to assess the pre-
cise role played by this new evangelical force, is the institutional
framework in which it was produced and in which it operated.

Pietism was not simply a reaction against a prevailing theology; it was also a product of the difficulties inherent in the
established character of New England Puritanism and of institutional difficulties which long antedated the Great Awakening.
Indeed, the revival itself was in large measure an attempt by
the standing clergy of New England to resolve ecclesiastical
problems without altering the basic structure of such institutions as the halfway covenant and the parish system. The radical pietism resulting from the revival, moreover, was not a force
which by itself necessarily deeply damaged the Standing Order.
But when pietism was enabled—or even compelled—to join
forces with those struggling against the establishment over traditional parish issues (ministerial salaries, the location of meeting-
houses, the formation of new ecclesiastical societies), the result

was widespread disorder and disruption. Those institutional issues which had been common before 1740 continued to be the
usual ones after the Awakening, and with both pietists and
their neighbors battling the standing churches—albeit for different reasons—the establishment was considerably weakened.

By the beginning of the eighteenth century, the functions and
responsibilities of the civil arm of the establishment (the town,
parish, or society) and the spiritual (the church) had been de-
lineated, and for the most part, separated. The church alone
made decisions on all questions relating to membership, from
eligibility for baptism to criteria for admission to communion
to discipline for wayward members. It controlled the wording
of its articles of faith and covenant, decided under what platform of government it would operate, and selected its own
officers (pastors, deacons, and ruling elders, if any), although
its choice of minister had to be ratified by the parish, which
paid his salary. The parish held the power of the purse, since
it voted and collected ecclesiastical taxes. This not only meant
that it had a voice, technically the power of veto, in the selection of a minister, but also that it could in practice decide who
was to be exempt from taxation. It was the parish which built
and maintained the meetinghouse, and decided on its location.
In Connecticut, the creation of new parishes and the drawing
of parish boundaries were entirely in the hands of the provincial
legislature, although the parish could initiate requests for
changes and was usually asked to acquiesce in them. A gray
area of uncertainty between church and parish functions always
existed, but even where overlap was not itself an open point of
conflict, the close relationship of church and state made it inevitable that decisions of either had repercussions for the other.

An excellent illustration of the continuing interaction and relationship between basically religious difficulties within the
standing church (which after 1740 took the form of a struggle
over evangelical pietism) and the essentially civil difficulties
within the parish system is provided by the experience of the
First Church and Society of Norwich, Connecticut. The com-
motions in Norwich not only produced one of the most important leaders for the new Separate/Separate-Baptist denomina-

tions in Isaac Backus, but they offer an opportunity for a de-
tailed case study of the background of the Great Awakening,
its impact in church and parish, and the blending of the traditional institutional problems of the standing churches with the
new evangelical pietism produced by the Great Awakening.

The town of Norwich was founded in 1660 by settlers from
Saybrook, Connecticut, under the leadership of the Reverend
James Fitch, who became its first minister. The Indian purchase which constituted the town lands was nine miles square—
a rather large area—but until 1716 the town remained a single
parish or society for ecclesiastical purposes. Apparently, the
Saybrook settlers brought their church organization with them,
but in the absence of church records under Fitch, little is known
of the early practices of the church. The only church document
extant is a covenant, owned by the congregation in 1675/6 at
the time of King Philip's War. Fitch suffered a stroke in 1694,
and the church negotiated for nearly six years before obtaining
the services of John Woodward, who was ordained in October
of 1699.

A bit more is known about the church under Woodward, although the records, with the exception of the admitting of members and baptisms, are not very full. If Woodward did not introduce the halfway covenant, he practiced it from the beginning of his ministry, keeping separate lists of covenant owners
and those admitted to full communion. The use of double lists
was not surprising, since the point of the halfway covenant (recommended by a synod in 1662) was to permit those baptized
in infancy who had not yet evidenced the necessary qualifications for sainthood to have their children baptized following an
intellectual rather than "gracious" affirmation of the doctrines
of the church as contained in its covenant. A few disciplinary
cases are also recorded, but most of the records have not survived. Woodward's ministry was a troubled one, as he had difficulty with the church over the 1675/6 covenant, and with the
town (or society) over the Saybrook Platform, the location of a
new meetinghouse, and his salary.

The dispute with the church was resolved in 1709 by a church
vote which, in effect, repudiated the covenant of 1675/6. Wood-

ward thereafter had the support of the majority of his church, as was usually the case in ministerial disputes in the eighteenth century. The source of Woodward's serious difficulties—again, typically—was the town acting as an ecclesiastical society. A battle over the location of the meetinghouse lasted from 1709 to 1713, and was settled only with the creation of a new society in the west part of the town in 1716, the first of seven new societies carved out of the original town tract by 1761. Adding to the acrimony caused by this struggle and undoubtedly related to it was the steady refusal of the society from 1711 to increase Woodward's salary or even to pay his present one; this conflict was not resolved until five years after his dismissal by a court judgment favorable to the minister. Complicating the town's attitude toward financial support was its opposition to the Saybrook Platform, produced by a council in 1708 of which Woodward was a scribe. The Platform, which the Connecticut legislature had converted into law in October 1708, called for county associations of ministers to supervise the churches, ordain ministers, and hear disputations within the churches. It was an attempt by the colony to enforce ecclesiastical uniformity, orthodoxy, and tranquillity, although to many it seemed destructive of congregational autonomy and basically Presbyterian. The legislature did permit churches and societies to register dissent from the Platform, however, and hence not be bound by it. A large part of Woodward's trouble apparently lay in his failure to inform his people of this proviso.

Several points of interest may be noted with regard to Norwich's opposition to Woodward and the Saybrook Platform. Although a majority of the church sustained the minister, one member—Joseph Backus, the grandfather of Isaac Backus—led a separation from the church. Backus was unable to gain victory, however, until he won the support of the ratepayers in society meeting, which proved possible because of meetinghouse difficulties and the question of subdivision of the society. Once the issue had changed from religious to civil, the position of the church majority became hopeless, for the adult male members of the church were completely outnumbered in society meetings. The merging of such problems as parish boundaries, meeting-

house location, and salary, with intra-church difficulties thus began early in Norwich, and the difficulties of John Woodward,
long before the Awakening, presaged those of his successor,
Benjamin Lord, after the revival. If there were lessons to be
learned by Woodward's successor, they were that he could nor-
mally expect the support of the church in times of trouble, but
that this backing was meaningless within the parish so long as
only a small proportion of the ratepayers were church members.

Benjamin Lord was ordained on November 20, 1717, and
remained minister to the First Church and Society until his
death in 1784 (for the last seven years the church had a younger
associate pastor). Lord's ministry of sixty-seven years was one
of the longest in eighteenth-century New England, but it was
not always smooth sailing. His pastorate can be divided into
four distinct phases: the first, from his ordination to 1740, was
a period of superficial peace underlaid with many potentially
dangerous and unresolved difficulties; the second, from 1741 to
1744, encompassed the years of the revival; the third, from
1744 to 1767 saw years of strife within church and society;
the fourth, from 1767 to his death, was a period of tranquillity
and peace.

The first phase of Lord's ministry, though superficially a
period of harmony in church and society, saw many of the
seeds of division sown that later helped produce twenty years
of conflict in Norwich. Within the church, the major problems
were those of church membership and church discipline (particularly with reference to the Saybrook Platform). Within the
society, there were continual pressures from inhabitants of out-
lying areas to establish their own parish and church for more
convenient and immediate religious service and more accessible
schooling. Reducing membership and tax revenue within the
societies by the creation of new ones rendered the payment of
ministerial salaries more difficult, particularly in a period of
continuous inflation. None of these potentially volatile issues
exploded until late in 1744 or early in 1745, but they were
building up during the first period of Lord's ministry. Although
Benjamin Lord was spared open confrontations with his congregation before the Great Awakening, other ministers in New

England were not so fortunate. These ecclesiastical difficulties were hardly symptomatic expressions of a society anticipating a great revival; rather, they were perennial conflicts over the issues which mattered in rural New England: finances, power, and local convenience. . . .

For a variety of quite understandable reasons, Benjamin Lord was favorably disposed to the notion of a large-scale revival of religion in his church and society. Full membership in the church would be increased and halfway members brought to the communion table by the only means conceivable within the covenant theology—a satisfactory conversion experience which could be related to the church. Those inhabitants of the society who stood in no adult relation to the church would be brought under its watch and care, and if there were sufficient numbers of adult male ratepayers among those revived, problems over money might justifiably be expected to vanish. Within the limitations of accepted theology and church practice, therefore, Benjamin Lord attempted to foster revival. This was behind [a] decision to join the town's ministers in the public lectures introduced in 1727/8, which he hoped would mean "that vital practical Religion may really revive in the midst of us, That a Spirit of prayer and Conversion may be abundantly poured out on the rising and risen Generation." If perhaps it led to [a] decision to employ written relations, it was certainly behind [a] trip to Northampton to consult with Jonathan Edwards, who was having great success with "harvests" in that town, and it led him to embrace the evangelists who came in the wake of George Whitefield's 1740 journey to New England. The latter, Benjamin Lord fervently hoped and undoubtedly prayed, were the answer to his needs.

Although Whitefield did not stop at Norwich on his first tour, other evangelists did. Some, standing ministers like Jonathan Parsons and Eleazer Wheelock, who had discovered their ability to rouse the people, were invited or embraced by Benjamin Lord. Others, like James Davenport, came anyway. The result was what Lord in June of 1743 described (with eleven other ministers in his area) "as a great and glorious work of divine grace, and a great reformation of religion." In Norwich First

Church, thirty-five males and fifty-six females joined the church
in full communion between 1741 and 1744, including the first
Negroes and Indians admitted to full membership. Of this total,
twenty-eight had been halfway members for an average of
twelve years—twice as long as those halfway members joining
the church in full communion before 1741. In the same four-
year period, only thirty-four owned the covenant and became
halfway members. And for the first time in Lord's ministry,
he was not only paid what he considered was an equitable
salary, but was actually overpaid for the years 1742, 1743, and
1744!

The revival was not without its problems. In 1741, the church
agreed to cooperate in choosing delegates to the "general Convention att Gilferd, for the promoting of the General Harmony
and Peace of the Churches in this Colony," with the proviso
"that it dont Infringe the Liberty, which we may Claim by the
former Dissent from the Established Form of Discipline in the
Government." The meeting at Guilford produced recommendations to prevent what many Connecticut ministers considered
revival abuses—particularly lay exhorting and itinerant preaching—which were translated by the legislature into law in 1742.
These itinerants—many uneducated religious extremists in one
sense or another—were held by many pro-revival ministers like
Lord to be responsible for the excesses of some of their people,
who were "so Imposed upon . . . and so Infatuated by [a]
Strange kind of Spirit as to think (Many would think) there
was much of the Spirit of God" in their actions. Lord took
notes and affidavits of some of these "dreadful" happenings, as
when one Nathaniel Lothrop, Jr., challenged "all the apposers to
say that I have not got the spirit of god in me for i know . . .
striking hand on his breast that I have," and continued that "it
would be pleasentis sight that ever my eyes saw if Christ would
come in the cloud and take vengeance on all the workers of
iniquity this night and to hear Christ give a commission to the
devils to drag your soul down to heel, my dear sister Anne."
Lothrop and others like him were, from Lord's point of view,
guilty of what those at the time called "antinomianism and
censoriousness."

Unfortunately, not all the people held views as patently erroneous as those of Nathaniel Lothrop, Jr. Much more dangerous to Lord were the large numbers of honest, God-fearing,
and sober folk in his church who, having had an immediate
crisis conversion experience themselves, began to doubt the
saintliness of those of their fellows who could not prove a
similar experience, although they had been admitted to full
membership in the church. Equally dangerous was the fact that
the revival had hit hard in the farthest corners of the society,[17]
where Lord could not so easily counteract the extremist views
of the converts, where he could not so easily dispute with or
keep out the itinerants, and where large numbers of ratepayers,
having acquired religious zeal, came to desire more convenient
worship and their own pastor close at hand. Lord's attempt to
encourage what he considered to be genuine revival while opposing its excesses was both difficult to practice and to compre-
hend, and he seemed to many zealots to be an "opposer" of
true religion. By 1744, when only five people joined the church
in full communion, it was clear that the revival itself was
played out. What remained to be dealt with was the growing
hostility of many to Lord and his church.

Although hints of difficulty had appeared before, the first
clear-cut evidence of dissension within the church appeared at
a meeting on December 13, 1744, convened to consider routine
disciplinary action against a wayward brother accused of drunkenness. Deacon Hezekiah Huntington made a motion "that the
Pastor in Some Convenient Time would Give the Church an
account of their Former Settlement, Since, there Appeared Some
who were Uneasy about the Matter of Discipline in the Church,
who might be So, thro Ignorance of what had been done as to
the Settlement of that matter, before they were admitted Members." In his acceptance of this motion, Lord noted that only
four members of the church remained who had been members
at his ordination and that several members had been uneasy
about the disciplinary case under consideration "under a Pretence That They didn't Know what Foundation the Church
Stood upon."

[17] That is, in the farther geographic corners, farther from Lord's church.

On January 10, 1745, Lord delivered a long address to the
brethren of the church which he called a "Representation of
the Settlement of the Church and State thereof from the Year
1717 . . . together with a History of the Pastors Proceeding
Agreeably Thereto." He rehearsed the steps by which the
church "chose to be directed (as to humane Forms) by the old
Platform drawn up in 1648," pointed out that he had consulted
the church on every point of action he had taken which might
threaten the church's independence (his attendance at the
county association, the weekly lectures, the Guilford meeting),
and argued that all steps had been taken with full protection
for the church's liberty. The church chose a committee to consult with the pastor "to forward the Business of the Next Meeting," and adjourned to February 20, 1745.

What the business of the next meeting was to be was clarified
on February 19, 1745, when the committee met to consider
action to be taken in view of the withdrawal from communion
of Hugh Calkins and Jedidiah Hide, and decided to recommend to the church that it send representatives to ascertain the
reasons for the separation. Because of the faulty chronology of
later accounts of the separation in Norwich, it is important to
note that it had begun *before* the critical meeting of February
20, 1745, at which, according to the church records, the church
voted that "tho it is Esteemed a desirable thing, That Persons
who Come into Full Communion, offer some publick Relation
of their Experiences; Yet we do Not judge nor hold it, as a
Term of Communion." The evidence indicates that this vote
by itself was not as responsible for separation as Isaac Backus
and others later suggested. Indeed, it seems likely that the
causal sequence was just the reverse of that usually given. Instead of abolition of relations followed by separation, there was
separation followed by abolition of relations. The best explanation for this seems to be that Lord (and a large majority of
the church) had decided that the errors of the revival made it
plain that relations did not necessarily make true saints. Many
of those who could relate satisfactory conversion experiences
had very probably undergone sudden psychological crises which
Lord held (in company with Jonathan Edwards) were not really
"gracious" at all. Lord had already told one of those separating

that he lacked true grace. Separation only confirmed the analysis, for genuine saints would not absent themselves from communion. For their part, the Separates were in reality less agitated about the abolition of relations than about the fact that many who had joined the church before the revival had, during the Awakening, experienced conversions of a far different nature from those which the church had always accepted as evidence of grace. This led Hugh Calkins to later argue that "he was received into this Church when he was unconverted". . . .

As the Norwich First Church struggled with religious separates within its body, the Norwich First Society began facing the first of a long series of attempts to subdivide it, or at least make public worship more accessible to more of the society's ratepayers. The two debates were not unconnected. On April 15, 1745, a petition was sent to the General Assembly from forty individuals, predominantly inhabitants of the westerly part of the First Society, requesting "a Distinct Ecclesiastical Society with Township Privileges" for their section. The petitioners alleged that they were "so scituate as to Render . . . Attendance on the Publick Worship of God in the several Societys" to which they belonged "exceeding Difficult, som of us Living more than six miles Distant from our Respective Places of Publick worship and the ordinary badness of the way together with the Extraordinary Difficulties of the winter and spring seasons Renders it impractical for us with our families many of which are numerous to attend on Divine worship as we would Gladly Do." The petition was headed by the signatures of William Lothrop and Samuel Leffingwell, two of the separatists against whom the church was instituting disciplinary action by July of the same year. Both men were among those who offered their reasons for separation in August of 1745. Their efforts at seeking a distinct society reinforce the conclusion that, because of their obvious new light dislike of Benjamin Lord, they were seeking to separate from the First Church but not necessarily from the Connecticut ecclesiastical establishment.

The petition of 1745 was unsuccessful, but the strength of the so-called "Separates" after they had organized their own church remained in the westerly section of town which consid-

ered itself geographically ill-served by Lord's First Church.
There were sporadic efforts thereafter to gain a distinct society
in the area, which were supported and even instigated by those
who had separated from the First Church. Almost from the
very beginning of Benjamin Lord's difficulties with church and
parish, it becomes difficult to distinguish between opponents motivated predominantly by evangelical pietism and those motivated by other reasons. Those clearly identifiable as radical
pietists, totally opposed to the parish system, constituted a
minority of the adherents of the "Separate" position.

By October 17, 1745, the First Church had given those withdrawing from communion "time to consider of the Warning . . .
given of their Separation, which hath been Judged by the
Church to be unwarrantable and a disorderly Walking," and
declared that eight of these individuals—Jedidiah Hide, William
Lothrop, Samuel Leffingwell, Joseph Griswold, Isaac Backus,
John Leffingwell, Jr., Phoebe Calkins, and Elizabeth Backus—
were not fit to "have Communion with the Church, while they
manifestly withdraw from, and refuse to have Communion
therewith." Therefore, the church suspended them "from the
Communion thereof in Special ordinances; till they Shall receive better Light and manifest their desire to Return to the
Communion thereof with proper Reflections on their past Conduct in Seperating therefrom." That those withdrawn were suspended rather than excommunicated can be viewed as indica-
tive of the conciliatory attitude of Benjamin Lord. But it also
demonstrates that Lord and the church saw this separation not
as the first step in the creation of a new denomination outside
the standing churches but as a family quarrel within it, not one
susceptible of immediate settlement, perhaps, but of ultimate
solution—on the church's terms, of course. Excommunication
was for those clearly beyond the pale in doctrine or practice,
while suspension was preferable for those unreconciled but re-
concilable.

Disciplinary action against members withdrawing from communion continued into 1746. One of those heard by the church
in August offered as a reason for separation "the method of
admitting adult persons to Baptism, and of Baptized persons

owning the Covenant, and of children to Baptism," the first objection to the halfway covenant recorded in Norwich. None of those heard in 1746, any more than those a year earlier, complained of the system of church establishment. But those separated from Lord constituted the hard core of the Bean Hill Church organized July 16, 1746, in the westerly section of town, and one of their number—Jedidiah Hide—was ordained its first pastor on October 30, 1747.

Those withdrawn from the First Church (a total of twenty individuals) were hardly sufficient to produce a thriving and viable competing church. But soon after Hide's ordination, the First Society began to talk about constructing a new meetinghouse, and in the ensuing debate over its location and the ultimate decision to build the new house in the eastern end of the society, the Bean Hill Church made gains. The issue of the location of the new meetinghouse was first raised in 1748, presumably by west-enders who had long been complaining of their difficulties in attending public worship. The society appealed for a committee of the legislature in May of 1748 to fix the spot, the decision being to build again at the same place. This proved unsatisfactory to the east-enders, who petitioned the assembly for redress, arguing that the location was "neither in the Center of the Society, or in the Center of the Inhabitants Travel, or Interest that must build and support the Same." A location more favorable to the east-enders resulted, but left those on the west side of the society (where a separate church was in existence to provide more accessible worship) even more unhappy. The west-enders had failed to gain a division of the society in 1745, and now had not only failed to win a more favorable location for the meetinghouse, but were faced with one less conveniently situated than before. Under the circumstances, it was not surprising that many began to drift into attendance at the Bean Hill Church, motivated not necessarily by the pietistic leanings of the minister, but by his geographical convenience. This was always one of the chief assets of the Separates; they could fulfill demands for accessible worship, since they were not bound by the structural inflexibilities of the parish system.

The difficulties over the location of the meetinghouse and its construction, combined with the creation of the Bean Hill Church and the establishment of a new society in 1751 (the Sixth, or Chelsea Society, taken from the southern part of the First Society), produced financial problems for Benjamin Lord. The construction of the new meetinghouse was an expensive proposition (although largely financed by private subscription), and many ratepayers were hostile to Lord either because of their extreme new light proclivities or because of pique over the problem of convenient worship. At first, the opposition to Lord was confined largely to the west-enders, among whom were eight pietistic Separates sufficiently committed to prefer jail to paying rates for the support of Benjamin Lord. The minister's salary was considerably underpaid in 1751 and 1752, and in 1753 the society was forced to appeal to the assembly because of inability to choose collectors for the west end of the parish. The west-enders were apparently able to enlist sufficient sympathy in society meetings to prevent rates being collected in their part of the society. As Isaac Tracy—a west-ender, frequenter of the Bean Hill Church, and one of the town's deputies to the assembly—put it in one society meeting called to choose a collector: "it want worth a while to be meallimouth'd about it for I suppose the Major part of this meeting dont want any Collector nor are willing to pay money to wone who Cares nomore for one third part of the Society than if they were a Company of wolfs." Society resentment against Lord built up, partly because of the sufferings of the imprisoned Separates, partly because of the appeal to the assembly to choose a collector, and partly because he was now complaining about his back salary. This ultimately proved to the advantage of the Bean Hill Church.

By December of 1755, the society was willing to consider exempting from rates those "that are Commonly Called Separates by Reason of their withdraw from the Established Worship by the laws of the Colony in Said Society" and who "set up the publick Worship of God among them Selves according to their Consciences." Ratepayers qualifying totalled sixty-four names. How many of these were radical New Lights opposed to Lord, his church, and the Standing Order for religious reasons and how many were simply seeking more convenient worship is not clear. The action did not solve the salary dispute, however. In 1756, the society "altogether neglected to pay him, said Mr. Lord, for his service," and Lord was forced to petition the assembly for his money. Having received the support of the legislature, Lord gave in and agreed to accept for the future a reduced salary supplemented by voluntary contributions; he also gave up his insistence upon back salary. This compromise apparently reduced the friction between the minister and his congregation, but did not solve the problem of the west end which had contributed so greatly to provoking the salary dispute.

That many of the west-enders were still not opposed to the parish system is shown by a petition of December 1758 which the First Society received from eighty-six "Inhabitants and Dwellers in the westerly Part of said Society" requesting "(for reasons that are wele known by you) that said Society may be Divided Into two Ecclesiastick Societys." Of the signers of this petition, only thirty-two had been listed by the society in 1755 as "Separates." Many of those pietists who had withdrawn from the First Church did not sign, but Hugh Calkins, John Leffingwell, Jr., Samuel Leffingwell, and William Lothrop did. The petition was also signed by John Fuller, who was ordained a few months later as pastor of the Bean Hill Church. Fuller had previously been considered as a candidate for minister of the Sixth Society and later returned to the Standing Order as minister at Plainfield; his influence in generating this petition may have been considerable.

The proposal to subdivide the First Society was not accepted, but the society did agree that those who "have Dissented and Withdrawn from the Stated Publick Worship and Ministry in Said Sociaty for some Time Past and Still Continue so to do and have Built a Meeting House, attend and Suport the Publick Worship and Ministry among them selves agreedable to their own Sentiments in Religious Matters," including those "who ware Members in full Communion with the Church in Said first Society" and "have withdrawn from Communion with Said

Church, Not agreeing with said Church, either in Principles or
in Practice in Matters Relating to Discipline in said Church,"
along with all others who in future desired to support this separate church (and publicly so declared, entered their names
with the society clerk, and constantly attended separate worship) would "be Released from Paying any Rate or Tax that
shall be by said first Society granted for Building or Repairing
any Meeting House for Divine Service, or for Settling or Sup-
porting the Ministry in said Sociaty." Of the seventy-nine individuals listed with this vote, forty-nine had signed the 1758
petition for a distinct society, and thirty had not. Perhaps
equally important, thirty-seven signers of the 1758 petition were
not interested in 1759 in being released from their financial obligations to the First Society in order to attend the Bean Hill
Church; these thirty-seven had apparently merely desired more
convenient public worship within the existing parish system. The
1758 petition, therefore, represented the joint effort of over half
the First Society's ratepayers commonly in attendance at the
Bean Hill Church and large numbers of ratepayers who fre-
quented Benjamin Lord's church to gain a new standing society
and church in the westerly part of the First Society. It is very
significant that such a large proportion of Bean Hill "Separates"
had no objection to the parish system and its implications—
ministerial and meetinghouse rates—provided they were raised
for a church and minister satisfactory to them, and that a large
number of adherents of the standing church had no objection
to joing forces with the "Separates" in this effort to subdivide
the parish.

The 1758 petition and the subsequent creation in 1759 of
what was in effect a poll parish for those attending the Bean
Hill Church together indicate rather clearly the ways in which
the interests and principles of a number of different groups of
people could overlap to disrupt the establishment. One group
of Bean Hill adherents—holding a position of extreme separatism including the doctrine of the separation of church and
state—refused to sign the 1758 petition. Another group of Bean
Hill adherents—virtually indistinguishable in their pietism from
the separationists—was willing to seek entrance into the Stand-

ing Order. This faction tended to merge in interests with a group less radical in its religious outlook, but certainly desirous of more convenient worship than that provided by Benjamin Lord's church and willing to seek it with the Bean-Hillers. On the question of the subdivision of the society, these latter two groups joined forces with a number of ratepayers not at all interested in attending the Bean Hill Church unless it was clearly recognized as part of the religious establishment.

Following the society's decision to exempt the Bean-Hillers from ecclesiastical taxes, Benjamin Lord's relations with his ratepayers improved considerably, and by 1767, when he preached a sermon commemorating his fifty years at Norwich, peace and harmony again reigned. Lord was, after all, a very old man, and his last years were unquestionably eased emotionally if not financially in 1767 by his decision to receive his salary entirely by voluntary contribution rather than by rate. The Bean Hill Church failed to prosper after 1760; Gamaliel Reynolds replaced John Fuller as pastor and became an Antipedobaptist in 1766. After this, many of the Bean-Hillers returned to worship with Benjamin Lord, some joined neighboring standing churches, and Reynolds celebrated the church's last communion service in 1772. The reunion of the "Separates" with the Standing Order and particularly with Lord was undoubtedly facilitated by his longevity, since he outlived nearly all those who had vehemently opposed him during and after the Great Awakening. Those few Bean-Hillers who were violently anti-establishment and pietistic probably joined Gamaliel Reynolds in embracing Antipedobaptism, but most of the church had probably never opposed the Standing Order on general principle, and with pietism dying and civil ill-feeling over meetinghouse, salary, and the formation of new societies far in the past, peace within the First Chuch and Society was possible.

A NOTE ON THE LITERATURE
OF THE AWAKENING

Although much has been written on the Great Awakening, there are few general assessments—a reflection of the sectional peculiarities that separate the course followed in the Carolinas, Virginia, the Middle Colonies and New England. Invariably generalizations are drawn from a particular area and extended elsewhere by extrapolation. This is the case with the most recent and provocative assessment, Alan Heimert's *Religion and the American Mind: From the Great Awakening to the Revolution* (Cambridge, 1966), which deals largely with New England, although it generalizes on the whole. (For comment on Heimert's very controversial book, see the contrasting reviews by William G. McLoughlin in *The New England Quarterly*, XL, 1967, and Edmund S. Morgan in *The William and Mary Quarterly*, Ser. 3, XXIV, 1967). The Awakening, by sections, is considered in Edwin S. Gaustad, *The Great Awakening in New England* (New York, 1957) and C. C. Goen, *Revivalism and Separatism in New England, 1740–1800* (New Haven, 1962)—the standard accounts; Leonard J. Trinterud, *The Forming of an American Tradition: A Re-examination of Colonial Presbyterianism* (Philadelphia, 1949)—very largely replacing Charles H. Maxson's *The Great Awakening in the Middle Colonies* (Chicago, 1920) as the standard account; and Wesley M. Gewehr, *The Great Awakening in Virginia, 1740–1790* (Durham, N. C., 1930)—the only extensive account.

Among key articles not utilized or mentioned in the text—their titles giving indication of their content—are H. B. Parkes, "New England in the Seventeen-Thirties" (that is, on the eve of the Awakening), in *The New England Quarterly*, III, 1930; Robert Sklar, "The Great Awakening and Colonial Politics: Connecticut's Revolution in the Minds of Men," in The Connecticut Historical Society *Bulletin*, XXVIII, 1963; Frederick B. Tolles, "Quietism versus Enthusiasm: The Philadelphia Quakers and the Great Awakening," reprinted in his *Quakers and the Atlantic Culture* (New York, 1960); Eugene E. White, "The Preaching of George Whitefield during the Great Awakening in America" and "The Protasis of the Great Awakening in New England," in *Speech Monograph*, XV, 1948, and XXI, 1954; Leonard W. Labaree, "The Conservative Attitude toward the Great Awakening," in *The William and Mary Quarterly*, Ser. 3, I, 1944; and the articles of Perry Miller—"The Great Awakening from 1740 to 1750," recently reprinted in his *Nature's Nation* (Cambridge, 1967), and, in his *Errand into the Wilderness* (Cambridge, 1956), "The Rhetoric of Sensation" and "From Edwards to Emerson." Several of Sydney Mead's articles put the Awakening in broad context: "Denominationalism: The Shape of Protestantism in America" and "American Protestantism during the Revolutionary Epoch," in *Church History*, XXIII, 1954, and XXII, 1953; "The Rise of the Evangelical Conception of the Ministry in America, 1607–1850," in H. Richard Niebuhr and Daniel D. Williams, eds., *The Ministry in Historical Perspective* (New York, 1956).

Theological currents are traced as they emerged from the Awakening by Joseph Haroutunian, in *Piety versus Moralism: The Passing of the New England Theology* (New York, 1932); H. Shelton Smith, in *Changing Conceptions of Original Sin: A Study in American Theology since 1750* (New York, 1955); and Conrad Wright, in *The Beginnings of Unitarianism in America* (Boston, 1955).

Among recent and better biographies of major figures of the Awakening and its aftermath are Stuart C. Henry, *George Whitefield: Wayfaring Witness* (New York, 1957); Charles W. Akers, *Called unto Liberty: A Life of Jonathan Mayhew, 1720–1766* (Cambridge, 1964); Edmund S. Morgan, *The Gentle Puritan: A Life of Ezra Stiles, 1727–1795* (New Haven, 1962); Louis Leonard Tucker, *Puritan Protagonist: President*

Thomas Clap of Yale College (Chapel Hill, 1962); and William G. McLoughlin, *Isaac Backus and the American Pietistic Tradition* (Boston, 1967).

The literature on Jonathan Edwards is, in itself, almost as large as the literature on the Awakening, and for this a convenient guide is to be found in Volume IV of James Ward Smith and A. Leland Jamison, eds., *Religion in American Life* (Princeton, 1961); this is Nelson R. Burr's *A Critical Bibliography of Religion in America.* But the best general biography is Ola E. Winslow's *Jonathan Edwards, 1703–1758: A Biography* (New York, 1941). Perry Miller's *Jonathan Edwards* (New York, 1949) is a sometimes difficult intellectual biography, subject to the criticism lodged by (among others) Peter Gay in *A Loss of Mastery: Puritan Historians in Colonial America* (Berkeley and Los Angeles, 1966) and Vincent Tomas in "The Modernity of Jonathan Edwards," *The New England Quarterly,* XXV (1952). Burr's bibliography of the Awakening can serve as a guide, although it is marred by a continuing acceptance of a direct link between German pietism and the American Awakening (a thesis disproved by Trinterud in *Forming of an American Tradition)* and by a degree of "old-fashionedness."

Joseph Tracy's *The Great Awakening: A History of the Revival of Religion in the Time of Edwards and Whitefield* (Boston, 1841) is old but, because of the extensive use of primary material, valuable. For the beginning student, however, particularly one interested in the intellectual aspects of the Awakening, the best introduction to the Awakeners' own writing is in Clarence H. Faust and Thomas H. Johnson, eds., *Jonathan Edwards: Representative Selections* (New York, 1935); H. Shelton Smith, et al., eds., *American Christianity: An Historical Interpretation with Representative Documents, 1607–1820,* Vol. I (New York, 1960); and the extensive and excellent collection edited by Alan Heimert and Perry Miller, *The Great Awakening: Documents Illustrating the Crisis and Its Consequences* (Indianapolis and New York, 1967).